שָׁלוֹם וּבְרָכָה

PRIMER EXPRESS

TEACHER'S EDITION

By
Ari Y. Goldberg
and
Nina Woldin

BEHRMAN HOUSE
www.behrmanhouse.com

TABLE OF CONTENTS

Published by Behrman House, Inc.
Springfield, NJ 07081
ISBN-10: 0-87441-776-7
ISBN-13: 978-0-87441-776-0
MANUFACTURED IN THE UNITED STATES OF AMERICA

Teacher's Edition Design: Itzhack Shelomi
Project Manager: Terry S. Kaye

INTENT AND PURPOSE OF *SHALOM UVRACHAH PRIMER EXPRESS*

Shalom Uvrachah Primer Express teaches Hebrew decoding skills while transmitting Jewish values. Its 96 pages are especially appropriate for schools with an hour or less of Hebrew instructional time per week. Students quickly and effectively learn to match Hebrew symbols and sounds, blend consonants with vowels, build syllables, and decode complete words.

Each of the 25 lessons introduces a carefully chosen Jewish cultural word—the key word—that enriches the student's cultural vocabulary while the student gradually develops a series of meaningful Hebrew decoding skills. In some cases, the key word may spark recognition of a concept from the student's background. This recognition will contribute to the student's sense of belonging to and feeling part of our rich Jewish cultural heritage. The key words, such as *mezuzah*, *baruch*, *mitzvah*, and *emet*, also serve as clues to help the student recall letter-sound and vowel-sound associations.

Based upon recent studies of Hebrew teaching methods, confusing letters are introduced separately and vowel sounds are carefully and systematically introduced in small manageable portions. Reading exercises provide extensive practice opportunity for each consonant and vowel. Numerous meaningful and challenging activities (e.g., Mix and Match, Name Know-How) offer additional learning opportunities for reading, writing, and exploring the Jewish cultural concepts.

At the same time, *Shalom Uvrachah Primer Express* provides a connection to modern Hebrew and to Israel in a feature that appears at the end of each chapter, called "Picture It in Hebrew." In this feature, an appealing photograph illustrates a modern Hebrew word, while a motivating activity allows the student to use the word in its appropriate context.

Note: The words in "Picture It in Hebrew" may include letters and vowels that the students have not yet learned at that point in the book; these words are presented for sight reading and whole word recognition only. Students can repeat the words after the teacher, can examine the words to find sounds they recognize, and later, can look back with pride when they have acquired the skills necessary to decode the entire word.

The following is a brief outline of the text's pedagogic features:

1. letter-sound association
2. vowel-sound association
3. visual discrimination of look-alike letters
4. auditory discrimination of sound-alike vowels
5. consonant blending
6. diagnostic evaluations
7. Jewish cultural enrichment
8. modern Hebrew enrichment

Shalom Uvrachah Primer Express has been designed to ease your students through the acquisition of Hebrew decoding skills, and to inspire and encourage them to want to learn more while instilling in them a sense of pride and joy in the acquisition of a Jewish cultural vocabulary.

HOW TO USE THE TEXTBOOK

Using the Teacher's Edition

This Teacher's Edition contains the entire text of the *Shalom Uvrachah Primer Express* textbook, reproduced in reduced size. The pages are annotated with suggested activities, teaching methods, and other information to assist you.

Keep in mind that students learn in different ways. The three primary ways are aural, visual, and tactile. Similarly, teachers teach in different ways. Don't feel obligated to use a method that does not feel comfortable with your teaching style. By the same token, remember that since students learn in different ways, you should vary your teaching methods. Feel free to repeat an activity or method that worked especially well for you and your students.

> The information and suggestions in this Teacher's Edition are intended to assist you in developing your own teaching plan. You do not need to follow every suggestion on every page. Rather, many different options are provided from which you can choose.

Pacing

Students differ in ability. Teachers differ in style. Schools differ in the number and length of class sessions scheduled each week. Ultimately, you must decide how to pace your class's progress through the text. The 25 lessons in *Shalom Uvrachah Primer Express* vary in length, but most should take only one class session to cover. A short but more difficult lesson may take more time than a longer, simpler lesson.

Remember that mastery of each new letter or vowel is of primary importance. You are building a foundation for the student's entire Hebrew school experience and beyond. Before advancing to a new lesson, each student should be able to decode all the letters and vowels learned in previous lessons, know their names, and be able to blend the sounds. Feel free to return to previous lessons to review a letter or vowel whenever necessary. By the time they reach the end of the book, students should be able to read whole words rhythmically and fluently.

Homework

Whether or not to give homework is a question that should be addressed to your school principal. Keep in mind that homework can provide students with additional contact, repetition, and reinforcement of what has already been learned in class. Homework should not be used as a tool to teach new information.

If you do give homework, *Shalom Uvrachah Primer Express* makes assigning homework easy. Built into each lesson are a variety of exercises that reinforce reading skills. Any one of these exercises can be completed for homework.

Be sure to review homework assignments during the following class session. Doing this reassures the students that their efforts were noted and were a worthwhile expenditure of time.

Family Education

A partnership between home and school can help your students reach their greatest potential in their Hebrew studies. Therefore, every effort should be made to facilitate this partnership with your students' parents.

- Send home a letter after the first class session to establish parent-teacher communication.
- You can also send home an *alef-bet* chart. Ask the parents to post it on the refrigerator so the student can mark off each letter after it has been learned.

Make sure to include the parents in a *Siyum Hasefer* celebration (see page xiv) when the students have finished learning all the letters.

SCOPE AND SEQUENCE

The chart below shows the order of letter and vowel introduction in *Shalom Uvrachah Primer Express.* You will see that the letters are not introduced in alphabetical order but are based on the presentation of key cultural terms. Vowel sounds have been carefully and systematically introduced in small manageable portions.

Lesson Number	Teext Page	Key Word	Letters	Vowels
1	4	שַׁבָּת	בּ ת תּ שׁ	◌ָ ◌ַ
2	10	שַׁמָּשׁ	מ	
3	13	כַּלָּה	ל כּ ה	
4	18	בְּרָכָה	ר כ	◌ְ
5	22	הַבְדָּלָה	ב ד	◌ֲ
6	27	וְאָהַבְתָּ	א ו	
7	31	צְדָקָה	ק צ	
8	35	מִצְוָה		◌ִי ◌ִ
9	38	שְׁמַע	ע	
10	41	נָבִיא	נ ן	
11	44	חַלָּה	ח	
12	47	עֲלִיָּה	י	
13	50	לְחַיִּים	ם	
14	54	תּוֹרָה		וֹ ◌ֹ
15	57	טַלִּית	ט	
16	60	אֱמֶת		◌ֱ ◌ֶ
17	63	פֶּסַח	פּ ס	
18	67	שׁוֹפָר	פ	
19	70	עֵץ חַיִּים	ץ	◌ֵי ◌ֵ
20	74	יִשְׂרָאֵל	שׂ	
21	77	חַג שָׂמֵחַ	ג	
22	81	קָדוֹשׁ		וּ ◌ֻ
23	85	מְזוּזָה	ז	
24	89	בָּרוּךְ	ךְ	
25	92	אָלֶף	ף	

Vowels

There are opposing opinions about whether or not the *names* of the vowels should be taught. The decision about whether to teach the vowel names should be guided by your school policy.

Below you will find a list of the vowels and their names.

Vowel Name	Vowel
kamatz	□ָ
pataḥ	□ַ
shvah	□ְ
ḥataf pataḥ	□ֲ
ḥirik	□ִי □ִ
ḥolam	□ֹ וֹ
segol	□ֶ
ḥataf segol	□ֱ
tsere	□ֵי □ֵ
shuruk	וּ
kubutz	□ֻ

TEACHING AIDS

Chalkboard

Use the chalkboard to introduce new letters, to drill the class on letter combinations, to demonstrate similarities and differences between letters, to answer questions, to play games, and to present assignments.

Remember to vary the way in which you use the chalkboard. This can be as simple as changing the chalk color or varying the size of the letters you write.

Draw a picture on the chalkboard to illustrate the lesson. (The less polished an artist you are, the more the class will love your drawings.)

Incorporate children's need for physical movement. Plan quick-paced exercises that involve coming to the board. For example, have students copy a word that you have written on the chalkboard. There is really nothing more special about writing on a chalkboard than on paper—unless you are a child. Coming to the front of the room and writing on the chalkboard is exciting to many students. If they enjoy using the chalkboard, let them do it.

Flannelboard

A flannelboard can be used with the entire class, with small groups, or by a single student. It saves writing time at the chalkboard and presents letters exactly as they appear in a printed book. It also offers students the opportunity to manipulate letters and to form whole words.

Flannelboards can be purchased at a school supplies store or may be easily constructed by covering a large piece of cardboard with flannel. You can make flannelboard letters by gluing a small piece of velcro or sandpaper onto the back of existing flashcards or by cutting flashcards out of rough-textured construction paper. Most flannelboard techniques will also work with a magnetic board.
The flannelboard can be used to introduce new letters and display them clearly. It is also useful for drill or review.

Alef-Bet Chart

The *alef-bet* chart reminds the class that its ultimate goal is to learn the entire *alef-bet*. Consider displaying several different *alef-bet* charts to enhance the feeling that Hebrew is an important aspect of the classroom routine.

Use the chart to introduce new letters, to compare the appearance of letters, and to demonstrate the progress the class has made.

Point to individual letters on the chart. Go around the room and have each child, in turn, pronounce the name and sound of the letter.

Say the sound of a Hebrew letter and ask a student to point to the letter or letters that have that sound, or say the name of a Hebrew letter and ask a student to point to the correct letter.

Select two students. Have one say the sound of a letter and the other point to the letter that has that sound.

Alef-Bet Flashcards

The clue to the most effective use of flashcards lies in their name—flash. How long is a flash? At first, a flash can take a long time. Our goal is not to reach any specific speed but to increase the given speed gradually. Flashcard drills are effective and their very pace can make them exciting, but like all drills, they can become boring. Variety helps to maintain interest.

There is a set of *alef-bet* flashcards available for use with *Shalom Uvrachah*, which can easily be used with *Shalom Uvrachah Primer Express*. Here are some ways to use these flashcards:

1. Hold the cards facing you and turn them around one at a time. Have each child identify the name and sound of the letter. Shuffle the cards and repeat, beginning with a different child, so that each child is given a turn with a new letter. Give each child several turns. For variety, after flashing for name and sounds separately, vary requests at random: e.g., name, name, sound, name, sound.

2. Put the cards into a bag and have each child take a turn fishing out a letter and giving its name or sound.

3. Distribute cards to each student. As you call out a name or sound, the student with the matching card holds it up.

4. Draw a tic-tac-toe grid on the chalkboard. Divide the class into two teams. Display a flashcard to team *alef*. If a student from team *alef* answers correctly, the student may write an *alef* in a square. Students from team *bet* do the same, using a *bet*. Keep playing until one team has three *alefs* or *bets* in a row. A "tournament" can be created by awarding the winning team one point. A new grid is drawn, and the game continues as long as you like.

5. Use a baseball theme. A correct answer to a displayed flashcard gets a team to first base. An incorrect answer is an out. A team with four correct answers has scored a run.

6. Distribute one flashcard to each student. Have students read their card silently and then hold it up. The first student, who has been given, let us say, a *gimmel*, says, "I packed my grandmother's suitcase, and in it I put a *gimmel*." The next student, who has been given a *bet*, says, "I packed my grandmother's suitcase, and in it I put a *gimmel* and a *bet*." The game continues in this manner. After everyone has had a chance, repeat the game but start in a different direction so those who had a few letters to read now have many. On this second round, students should be encouraged to quicken the tempo.

7. Display letter and vowel flashcards #1–7, for example, on the chalkboard ledge. Say, "I spy a *bet*" or "I spy an *'ah'* sound." Call on a student to come up and point to the card you "spied." Upon selecting the correct card, the student now has a turn to "spy" a card. The student then calls on a classmate to come up and find it.

Word Cards

There is a set of word cards available for use with *Shalom Uvrachah*, which can easily be used with *Shalom Uvrachah Primer Express*. These cards, printed on durable, heavy cardboard, include all Key and Heritage words covered by the book. (Each word card is numbered for easy reference to activities included in this Teacher's Edition.) The English meaning is on the back of each word card.

Word cards may be used by individuals or small groups of students, or by the class as a whole. Use the word cards to introduce the Key and Heritage words in each lesson. Also use the word cards for review.

1. Display a number of word cards on the edge of the chalkboard or in a pocket chart. Provide a clue about one of the words and have the student read

the correct word. For example, "This is the Jewish state" – *Yisrael.*

2. Distribute word cards to the class. Call out, one at a time, the words and phrases found on the individual cards. The student with the matching card supplies the correct answer by standing up, displaying the card, and reading the word or phrase.

3. Make a packet of ten word cards. The students sit or stand in a circle and pass the packet around while music is played on a tape or CD player. (Try to use Jewish or Israeli music.) When the music stops, the student holding the packet reads and/or translates the top card. This card is then placed at the bottom of the pile and the game continues in the same fashion.

4. Post two columns of word cards with six cards in each column. Individuals or teams choose a column. Taking turns, the students read the six Hebrew words. Then they switch and read the words in the other column. You can also play the game by translating the words.

5. Post a column of at least six words. Individuals or teams take turns "climbing up the ladder" by reading and translating the words on the ladder. Score one point for each word read correctly and two points for each word translated correctly. Then play again by reading the words in the opposite order to climb down the ladder.

6. Double sets of word cards (two identical cards for each word) can be used to play a memory game. After shuffling the cards, lay out sixteen cards (eight pairs of words) upside down, in rows. A student picks a card and reads it. He or she then tries to find its match. If successful, the student must then tell the meaning of the word in order to keep the pair. If the student defines the word incorrectly, or doesn't find the matching card, then the initial card is returned to its place face down.

Stopwatch and Tape Recorder

A stopwatch is an easy way to assess improvement in reading fluency. It can be used to time the speed at which a student reads a passage. Many students enjoy the experience of competing against their own best time.

The tape recorder also provides students with proof of their improvement. Record students as they read through a passage. Two or three weeks later have the students, in the same order, read the passage on a second tape. Then play back both and compare.

ALEF-BET FLASHCARDS AND WORD CARDS – MASTER LIST

A set of numbered *alef-bet* flashcards and word cards are available for use with *Shalom Uvrachah*. The same cards are compatible with *Shalom Uvrachah Primer Express*, although not all word cards are required. The following fifteen cards are not required in *Shalom Uvrachah Primer Express*: 2, 7, 8, 11, 13, 45, 46, 54, 55, 56, 57, 63, 64, 65, and 80.

Word Cards

1	שַׁבָּת	28	לְחַיִּים	55	אָמֵן
2	בַּת	29	אָדָם	56	סֵפֶר תּוֹרָה
3	שַׁמָּשׁ	30	יְצִיאַת מִצְרַיִם	57	נֵר תָּמִיד
4	כַּלָּה	31	תּוֹרָה	58	חָמֵץ
5	שַׁבָּת הַכַּלָּה	32	שַׁבַּת שָׁלוֹם	59	יִשְׂרָאֵל
6	בְּרָכָה	33	הַמּוֹצִיא	60	עֲשֶׂרֶת הַדִּבְּרוֹת
7	מַלְכָּה	34	רֹאשׁ הַשָּׁנָה	61	שִׂמְחַת תּוֹרָה
8	שַׁבָּת הַמַּלְכָּה	35	קָדוֹשׁ	62	חַג שָׂמֵחַ
9	הַבְדָּלָה	36	שָׁלוֹם	63	הַגָּדָה
10	וְאָהַבְתָּ	37	טַלִּית	64	מְגִילָּה
11	אָהֲבָה	38	יוֹם טוֹב	65	מָגֵן דָּוִד
12	צְדָקָה	39	שָׁנָה טוֹבָה	66	מָשִׁיחַ
13	קַבָּלַת שַׁבָּת	40	אֱמֶת	67	קִדּוּשׁ
14	מַצָּה	41	הַמּוֹצִיא לֶחֶם	68	סִדּוּר
15	מִצְוָה	42	אֲרוֹן הַקֹּדֶשׁ	69	יְהוּדִים
16	בַּר מִצְוָה	43	אֱלֹהִים	70	חֻמָּשׁ
17	בַּת מִצְוָה	44	פֶּסַח	71	יְרוּשָׁלַיִם
18	צִיצִית	45	כִּפָּה	72	אֵלִיָּהוּ הַנָּבִיא
19	קַדִּישׁ	46	מִשְׁפָּחָה	73	מְזוּזָה
20	הַתִּקְוָה	47	חֶסֶד	74	מַחֲזוֹר
21	שְׁמַע	48	שׁוֹפָר	75	מַזָּל טוֹב
22	עִבְרִית	49	נֶפֶשׁ	76	בָּרוּךְ
23	נָבִיא	50	תְּפִלָּה	77	מֶלֶךְ
24	חַלָּה	51	הַפְטָרָה	78	אָלֶף
25	הָרַחֲמָן	52	אֲפִיקוֹמָן	79	אָלֶף בֵּית
26	עֲלִיָּה	53	עֵץ חַיִּים	80	חַי
27	מִנְיָן	54	סֵדֶר		

Alef-Bet Flashcards

1	בּ	28	ם
2	תּ	29	וֹ
3	ת	30	◌ֹ
4	שׁ	31	ט
5	◌ָ	32	◌ֶ
6	◌ַ	33	◌ֱ
7	מ	34	פּ
8	ל	35	ס
9	כּ	36	פ
10	ה	37	◌ֵ
11	ר	38	◌ֵי
12	כ	39	ץ
13	◌ְ	40	שׂ
14	ב	41	ג
15	ד	42	וּ
16	◌ֲ	43	◌ֻ
17	א	44	ז
18	ו	45	ך
19	ק	46	ף
20	צ		
21	◌ִ		
22	◌ִי		
23	ע		
24	נ		
25	ן		
26	ח		
27	י		

TEACHING STRATEGIES

Key Words and Heritage Words

The words in *Shalom Uvrachah Primer Express* have been specifically chosen because they transmit some of the values and beliefs of our Jewish heritage. Introducing real words to the students is important because it assures them that learning Hebrew is more than just a process of decoding symbols.

Each lesson in *Shalom Uvrachah Primer Express* contains a "Key word"; an illustration representing the Key word appears at the top of each opening page. To facilitate discussion of the concepts related to the Key word, this Teacher's Edition contains guiding questions to be asked of the students.

Word cards containing both the Key and Heritage words can be a valuable tool for teaching new letters or vowels, facilitating drill work, and discussing concepts related to the Jewish cultural words. In addition, this Teacher's Edition provides supplemental exercises and activities to expand the students' understanding of the Key and Heritage words.

Here are some techniques for using the Key word to teach new letters and vowels:

1. Display the word card representing the Key word, write the Key word on the chalkboard, or have the students look at the Key word in their textbooks and then read the word to the class. If the students are familiar with any of the letters or vowels in the word, have the students identify them.
2. Discuss concepts related to the Key word and then point out the new letter or vowel being introduced.
3. If only one new letter or vowel is being introduced in the lesson, read the Key word to the students and ask the students to guess the sound of the new letter or vowel.
4. When using the textbook, have the students point to the new letter or vowel in the Key word.

New Letter and Vowel Introduction

Here are some techniques for introducing new letters and vowels:

1. Write the new letter on the chalkboard in print form.
2. Put the new letter on the flannelboard or magnetic board.
3. Pronounce the name and sound of the new letter or vowel and have the class repeat it in unison or individually.
4. Have students point to the new letter on the *alef-bet* chart and pronounce it.
5. When introducing a new letter, write a vowel the class already knows under the letter and ask the class to pronounce what you have written. Erase and change the vowels until you have used all the vowels the class knows. You can also follow a similar procedure using the flannelboard or magnetic board.
6. When introducing a new vowel, follow the procedure noted in #5 but instead combine the new vowel with different familiar letters.
7. Stress visual similarities with and differences from other letters or vowels.
8. Have the students form the letters or vowels out of pretzel sticks or licorice strips, and then enjoy the treat. You can also use nonedible materials such as pipe cleaners, yarn, ribbon, etc.

After you have introduced the new letter or vowel, have the students open their books to the new lesson. Introduce and practice the new letter or vowel before turning to the text, because children think of reading as something done from a book. If the difficult task of learning new material is done by using other teaching aids, then the task of reading—using the textbook—will be more rewarding.

Reading Techniques

There is no substitute for reading drill. The only way to produce fluent readers is to have them read and read, and then read some more.

If the class has read a page accurately, review the material with an eye toward increasing speed. If the class cannot read a page accurately, have them read it a second or third time. As a reminder to do this, every page of standard reading drill is prefaced by the phrase "Now Read & Read Again," along with the use of the recycling symbol.

Here are some techniques for making reading practice more interesting and varied in your classroom:

1. **Pairs.** Have students work in pairs reading lines to each other. Match a stronger reader with a weaker reader. Listen as they practice, correcting any errors that you hear.

2. **Random Selection.** Let the student roll a die or pick a number out of a hat. Whichever number comes up is the line the student must read.

3. **Songs.** Have the students try singing the sounds to the tune of a simple song such as "Twinkle Twinkle Little Star" or "Mary Had a Little Lamb." This works best with simple, single-syllable sounds.

4. **Echo Reading.** Divide the class into two groups, choosing from a variety of criteria: boys/girls; students with birthdays before July/after July; students wearing red/no red. One group is "reader" and the other is "echo." "Reader" reads a word or group of words and "echo" repeats the same word or words. Repeat the activity but switch "reader" and "echo."

5. **Tic-Tac-Toe.** Draw a tic-tac-toe grid on the chalkboard. Divide the class into two teams. To place an X or an O on the board, the students must correctly read a line in the book.

6. **Staccato Interruption.** Have a child read until you clap your hands. At that time, the next student reads. Determine the number of words according to the student's ability and reading fluency, keeping the pace lively.

7. **Choral Reading.** Have the first row of students read the first line in unison. Have the second row read the second line, and so on until all the lines have been read.

8. **Timed Reading.** Use a stopwatch to time reading. Students enjoy competing against their own best time.

9. **Student's Choice.** Allow each student the opportunity to read one line of his or her choice. Have the student identify the line number before reading. Another version is to have one student read a line and then call out another line number for the next student to read, or call out the name of the next reader.

10. **Team Reading.** Have four students work together to correct each other as members of the group take turns reading complete lines.

11. **Special Attention Words.** Call out a specific word, such as "line 3, fourth word," and have a child read that word. Have the child call out the location of the next one, or continue to call them out yourself with emphasis on words or letters that need extra attention.

12. **Responsive Reading.** Have students take turns reading one phrase at a time, with the class responding in unison.

13. **Odds and Evens.** Change the line sequence by first reading all the odd-numbered lines followed by the even-numbered lines.

14. **Finger Follow-Along.** Encourage students to concentrate by following the reading with their fingers.

15. **Stay Alert.** Keep students on their toes by calling on the same child more than once.

16. **Overlapping Words.** Have students read three words at a time. The first student reads three words. The second student overlaps by reading three words beginning with the second word. The third student begins with the third word, and so on. Another variation is to have the student begin with the previous student's last word.

17. **What's Missing?** Have one student read all the Hebrew sounds or words on a line, omitting one. Another student reads the sound or word that was skipped.

18. **Tape Recording.** Record students as they read a line. Two or three weeks later have the students read the same line, in the same order, on a second tape. Play back both tapes and compare.

19. **Dramatic Reading.** Legend has it that there was once a famous actress who was so talented that she was able to bring tears to the eyes of an audience simply by reciting the alphabet. Instruct the students to read a line of syllables dramatically, as if they were on stage. For example, suggest to the first person to read the line angrily; the second person should read sadly; and so on. A variation of this is to whisper a situation to the reader (e.g., you have just won a million dollars), and the class must guess the emotion the reader is trying to convey.

Picture It in Hebrew

The last page of each lesson in *Shalom Uvrachah Primer Express* contains a feature entitled "Picture It in Hebrew," with an appealing photograph, a modern Hebrew word for sight reading, and a short motivational English activity. The Hebrew word contains a new letter or vowel presented in the chapter and is meant for sight reading and whole word recognition only, not necessarily phonetic reading. Students will see the new letters and vowels they have learned in the context of "real" words used by Israelis and will begin to establish a connection to modern Hebrew language.

Online Workbook

Shalom Uvrachah Primer Express offers a companion online interactive workbook for Hebrew homework that kids will want to do! Students can go fishing and bowling on the computer, play bingo and tic-tac-toe, solve riddles, and even unlock Hebrew letter combinations while reinforcing Hebrew letters and vowels.

A personalized sign-up page asks students to create unique user names and passwords, allowing teachers to track their progress. Parents can follow along with their child's reading progress with printable transliterated PDF files in each chapter. *Shalom Uvrachah Primer Express* includes matching, circling, underlining, and drawing activities, but no formation of Hebrew letters. Instead, students can practice writing Hebrew with printable block print or script Hebrew writing exercises online. Visit www.behrmanhouse.com/suexpress to learn more about the *Shalom Uvrachah Primer Express* O*nline Workbook.*

Remediation

What should you do to remedy decoding problems? The strategy that you use depends upon the specific nature of the problem.

When students mispronounce words...
Read the word and have the class repeat ("echo") it.
Read the word again, slowly decoding each letter and vowel part.

When students are not reading fluently...
Have the students read into a tape recorder.
Tape-record a page and have individual students read along.
Use a stopwatch to encourage reading fluency.

When students lack confidence in reading...
Assign classmates for peer tutoring.
Group students of varying abilities together.
Encourage parental assistance.

When classwide errors occur...
Reteach the material.
Offer more class drill.
Reassess your teaching method.

When motivation to improve is needed...
Offer praise and encouragement.
Allow the students to act as teacher for a few minutes.
Give out stickers or small prizes.
Communicate with parents.

TIME MANAGEMENT

How to complete the book in one school year, teaching one lesson (or chapter) per week.

We recommend that your students spend a full year learning to read. Fluency and accuracy in Hebrew reading are important to their future success in Hebrew language study and to their sense of achievement in religious school.

One of the most difficult things to do when planning a curriculum is deciding exactly how to use the class time. Each class session should be divided into at least four distinct components.

1. Opening activity to review previous material or to set up the class session
2. Introduction of new material
3. Reinforcement of new material
4. Closing activity to summarize and reinforce the class session's content

The amount of time spent on each component will depend on the overall amount of time available for Hebrew instruction and on what you wish to accomplish. Creating a lesson plan in advance of every class session will help you to manage your time so that all your goals can be met.

If You Meet Once a Week for Hebrew Instruction...

If your school meets once a week for thirty weeks, on average you will need to complete one lesson per week. Keep in mind that some lessons will introduce two or three letters, while others will introduce only one. Therefore, some lessons will require more than one week of study, while other weeks you may be able to cover two lessons in one class session.

If You Meet Twice a Week for Hebrew Instruction...

If your school meets twice a week for thirty weeks, you can spend approximately two classroom sessions per lesson. Again, you will need to take into consideration the number of letters or vowels introduced in each lesson and pace your class accordingly.

To extend classroom time, assign work in the *Shalom Uvrachah Primer Express Online Workbook* to be completed at home.
Visit www.behrmanhouse.com/suexpress to learn more.

THE FIRST DAY OF SCHOOL

Setting the Stage

Before the first day of school, spend time planning the appearance of your classroom. The classroom should convey the message that Hebrew is exciting and important and that studying and learning Hebrew will be pleasant, worthwhile, and fun.

Play recordings of Israeli songs. Hang *alef-bet* charts and attractive Hebrew posters around the room. Display a selection of Hebrew books or anything else that contains Hebrew letters. Label classroom objects with their Hebrew names. Try to include both items of a religious nature (e.g., a haggadah, a *ḥallah* cover), as well as items from Israeli popular culture (e.g., soda labels, comic books). The appearance of your classroom is an important motivation for learning.

Introducing the Hebrew Language

Tell the students that they will be learning to read a language that is both very old and very new. The Torah, Judaism's oldest and holiest document, is written in Hebrew. Most of our prayers are written in Hebrew. But Hebrew is also a very new language. Up until the late 1800s, Hebrew was used only for ritual purposes. As the result of the creation of the State of Israel in 1948 and the adoption of Hebrew as Israel's official language, Hebrew has come to be used as a living, everyday language. For further information, *Journey Through Jewish History* by Seymour Rossel, available from Behrman House, has a section (pages 117–118) relating the amazing story of the father of modern Hebrew, Eliezer ben Yehudah, and the rebirth of the Hebrew language.

Hebrew Is Read from Right to Left

Demonstrate how to open a Hebrew book. Ask a student to come up and find the first page in a Hebrew book. Open a Hebrew book and point to where we begin reading on a page. Have an English and Hebrew phrase written on the chalkboard. Ask a student to come to the board and point to where one would begin to read each phrase.

Introducing the Textbook

Explain that in Judaism when we begin something new we say a special thank you to God by reciting a blessing. This blessing is called the Sheheḥeyanu. Lead the class in the recitation of the blessing.

בָּרוּךְ אַתָּה ה׳ אֱלֹהֵינוּ מֶלֶךְ הָעוֹלָם,
שֶׁהֶחֱיָנוּ וְקִיְּמָנוּ וְהִגִּיעָנוּ לַזְּמַן הַזֶּה.

Baruch atah Adonai Eloheinu melech ha'olam, sheheḥeyanu v'kiy'manu v'higiyanu lazman hazeh.

Praised are You, Adonai our God, Ruler of the universe, who has kept us in life, sustained us, and enabled us to reach this season.

Distribute the textbooks. Show the students the Hebrew letters on the cover. Allow a minute for the students to examine their new books, to flip through the pages, and to enjoy the colorful design. Then ask the students to open the book the "Hebrew way." Check to see that this is done properly.

Explain that there is a custom of eating something sweet on the first day of school so that learning will be a sweet and happy experience. Arrange to have candy, raisins, or other sweets to distribute to each child. Consider also having other treats, such as pretzels or popcorn, for students who may have special dietary concerns.

Tell the students that by the end of the year, they will be able to follow along in the *siddur* (prayer book) and *ḥumash* (Five Books of Moses) during synagogue services because they will know all the letters and vowels in the *alef-bet*!

Homework

The beginning of school is often a time of enthusiasm for the students, so now is the time when students are most eager to do homework. If you plan to assign homework throughout the year, give an assignment on the first day. This will also create the understanding and expectation that homework will be a regular part of their Hebrew learning experience.

Parent Participation

When parents are informed, students become more involved. When children sense their parents' interest, they become more motivated to achieve. On the first day of school, consider sending a letter home to parents, telling them about the important part they can play in their child's Hebrew studies. It will help you establish positive parent-teacher communication.

FYI

Some of your students may have had previous exposure to the Hebrew alphabet. Your students' Hebrew backgrounds need not affect your teaching methods, although they may affect how you pace the lessons.

SIYUM HASEFER

(Completing the Book)

When the class has finished *Shalom Uvrachah Primer Express*, it is time for a celebration. It is customary to hold a *Siyum Hasefer* upon the completion of a course of Jewish study.

Each year we finish reading our most important book, the Torah, and immediately begin reading it again. At this time we have a large celebration called *Simḥat Torah*. Traditionally, we have smaller celebrations when we finish studying other Jewish books. Such a celebration is called a *Siyum Hasefer*.

Include the students in the planning of the *Siyum Hasefer* so that they will feel that it is their celebration. Listed below are some appropriate activities that can be included:

- Invite the rabbi, cantor, education director, and parents.
- Recite the Sheheḥeyanu blessing.
- Serve refreshments accompanied by the appropriate blessings.
- Sing *Hatikvah* and other Hebrew songs.
- Play Hebrew team games.
- Present certificate of completion.

Make sure to create a lively, celebratory atmosphere in the classroom.

TABLE OF CONTENTS

READING PRACTICE

Have the students open their textbooks and tell them to look at the letter and vowel in the middle of the Key word (שַׁבָּת). Also ask the students to identify the sounds **["b" and "ah"]** and the name of the letter **[bet]**.

Point again to the *bet* on the chalkboard and add a *pataḥ* or *kamatz* under it. Ask students to sound out the letter and then the vowel, each separately, and then to combine the sounds of the letter and the vowel.

Read line 1 for the class. (Make sure the students are following along.) Repeat the line in unison with the class. Continue this procedure with line 2. For lines 3 and 4, have each student read one "word" at a time.

LESSON 1

Pages: 4–9
Key Word: שַׁבָּת
New Letters: בּ ת תּ שׁ
New Vowels: ◌ַ ◌ָ
Alef-Bet Flashcards: 1, 2, 3, 4, 5, 6
Word Card: 1

WELCOME TO HEBREW STUDY

Begin the class session by asking the students why the Hebrew language is important to the Jewish people. **[It is the language of the Jewish people. The Torah and many prayers are written in Hebrew.]**

KEY WORD – (שַׁבָּת)

What special things do we do on Shabbat? **[light candles, eat *ḥallah*, make Kiddush, eat special family meal together, go to services, etc.]**
When do we use Hebrew on Shabbat? **[during services or when reciting prayers for home rituals mentioned above]**

Have the students create English sentences that include the word Shabbat and share them with the class.

Display and read word card #1 (שַׁבָּת) or write this word on the chalkboard.

INTRODUCING THE NEW LETTER – בּ

Print a large *bet* on the chalkboard. Point to the letter *bet* on the chalkboard and on the word card and demonstrate its sound. Also point to the *bet* on the *alef-bet* chart posted in the room and have the students identify the letter's name and its sound.

INTRODUCING THE NEW VOWELS – (*KAMATZ*: ◌ָ and *PATAḤ*: ◌ַ)

Point to the *kamatz* and *pataḥ* on the *alef-bet* chart and demonstrate the sound that each vowel makes. Have the students repeat after you. Point to each vowel randomly and call upon a student to make its sound.

SEARCH AND CIRCLE

Read each sound on line 1 and then ask students what is different about the circled sound. For the other three lines, read the sounds and have the students circle the one sound that is different. Then call on students to explain their answers.

SOUNDS LIKE

Read the instructions to the class and then have the students complete the exercise independently. When everyone has finished, call on students to read each line and explain their answers.

INTRODUCING THE NEW LETTER – ת תּ

Display *alef-bet* flashcards #2 and #3 (תּ ת) next to each other, or write both these letters on the chalkboard. Teach the name and sound of the *tav*. How do these two letters differ? **[presence of dot]** Emphasize that both letters are pronounced the same way.

Have the students point to the key word (שַׁבָּת) in the textbook. Read the word. Ask the students to point to the ת in שַׁבָּת. Does the *tav* in שַׁבָּת have a dot in it? **[no]**

READING PRACTICE

Call on students randomly to read these two lines aloud.

FYI

The *tav* without a *dagesh* (dot) used to be pronounced differently by the Ashkenazic Jewish communities of Eastern Europe. However, modern Hebrew has adopted the Sephardic pronunciation (emanating from Spanish and Middle-Eastern communities), in which both versions of the *tav*—with or without a *dagesh*—are identical.

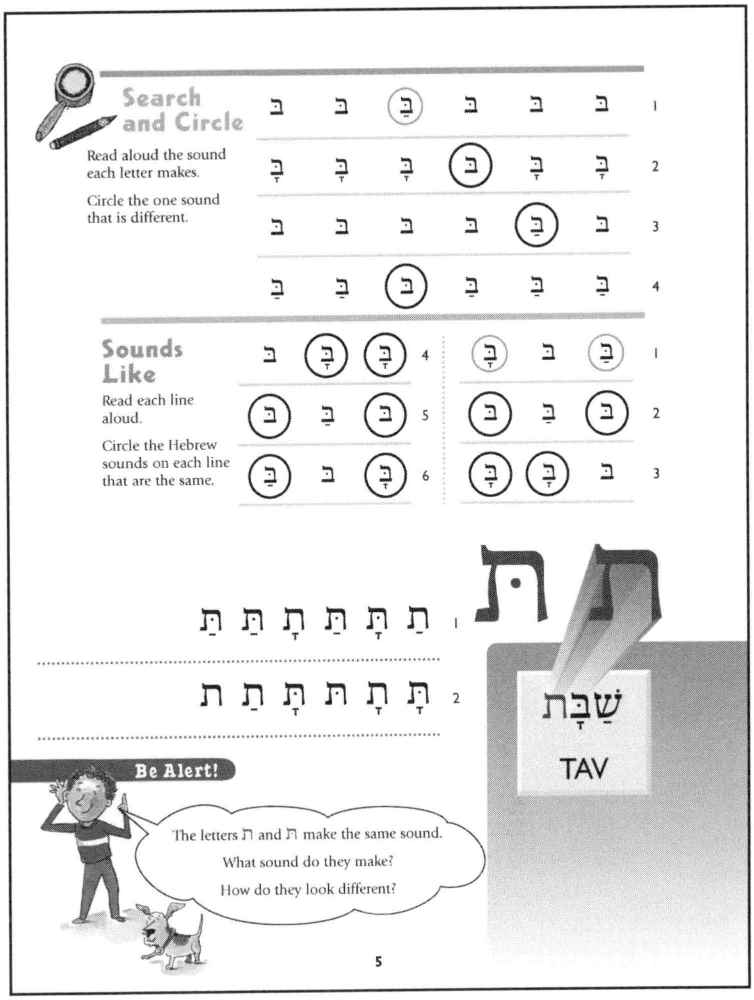

Search and Circle

Read aloud the sound each letter makes.

Circle the one sound that is different.

1 בּ בּ בּ בַּ בּ בּ

2 בָּ בָּ בּ בָּ בָּ בָּ

3 בּ בַּ בּ בּ בּ בּ

4 בַּ בַּ בַּ בּ בַּ בַּ

Sounds Like

Read each line aloud.

Circle the Hebrew sounds on each line that are the same.

1 בַּ בּ בָּ

2 בּ בַּ בּ

3 בּ בָּ בָּ

4 בָּ בָּ בּ

5 בּ בַּ בּ

6 בָּ בּ בַּ

תּ ת

1 תַ תָּ תַּ תָ תַּ תַּ

2 תָּ תָ תּ תָּ תַ ת

שַׁבָּת

TAV

Be Alert!

5

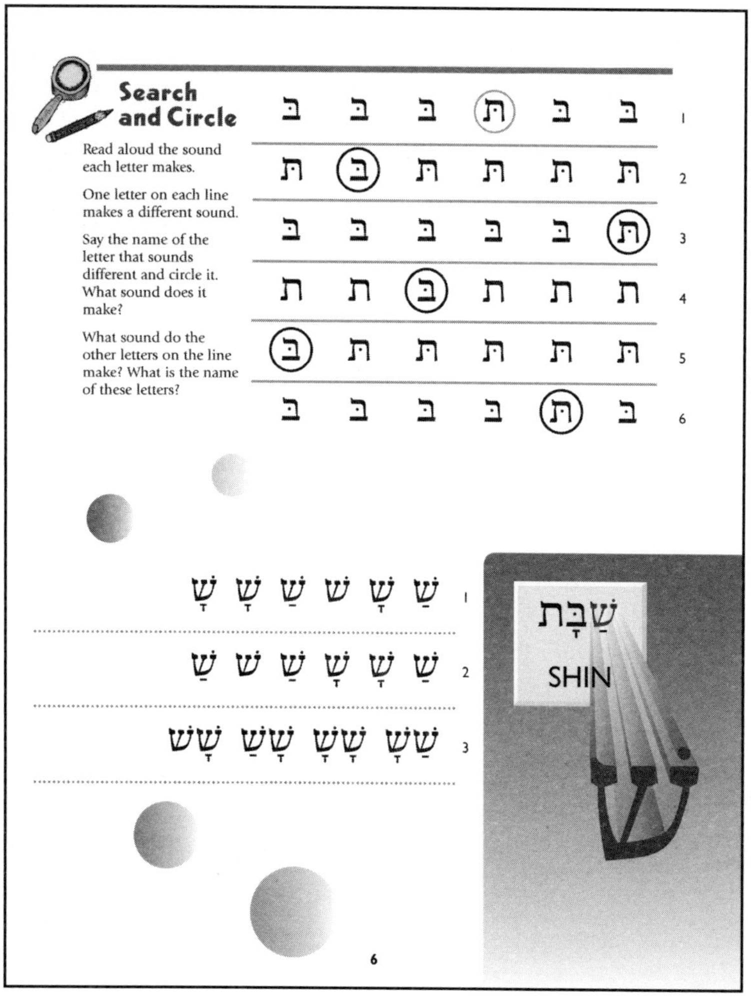

Search and Circle

Read aloud the sound each letter makes.

One letter on each line makes a different sound.

Say the name of the letter that sounds different and circle it. What sound does it make?

What sound do the other letters on the line make? What is the name of these letters?

1 בּ בּ (תּ) בּ בּ בּ

2 תּ תּ תּ תּ (בּ) תּ

3 (תּ) בּ בּ בּ בּ בּ

4 ת ת ת (בּ) ת ת

5 תּ תּ תּ תּ תּ (בּ)

6 בּ (תּ) בּ בּ בּ בּ

1 שַׁ שָׁ שׁ שַׁ שָׁ שָׁ

2 שַׁ שָׁ שָׁ שַׁ שׁ שַׁ

3 שַׁשָׁ שָׁשָׁ שָׁשַׁ שָׁשׁ

שַׁבָּת

SHIN

6

SEARCH AND CIRCLE

Read each sound on line 1 and then ask the students what is different about the circled sound. For the other five lines, have the students complete the exercise independently. (The teacher should not read the sounds aloud.) Then call on students individually to identify the name and sound of the letter that differs from the others. Call on another student to identify the name and sound of the other matching letters on the line.

INTRODUCING THE NEW LETTER – שׁ

Print the letter *shin* on the chalkboard and teach its name and sound. Emphasize the location of the dot – on the top right of the *shin*. Have a student come to the *alef-bet* chart and point out the *shin*. Display word card #1 (שַׁבָּת) and have a student point out the *shin* in the word and read the word.

READING PRACTICE

Read lines 1 and 2 in unison. Then read line 3 to the class and call on students at random to repeat the line.

NOW READ & READ AGAIN

Call on students at random to read each of the lines. Keep students on their toes by sometimes calling on the same child more than once. Don't forget to recycle this section. Repeat it as many times as you find helpful.

Now Read & Read Again

1 בָּ בַּ בּ בַּ בָּ בּ

2 תָּ תַּ תּ תָּ תַּ תּ

3 שַׁשׁ שַׁב שָׁת שָׁשַׁ שָׁבַ שָׁתָ

4 בַּשׁ תָּשׁ בַּת שַׁתַּ בָּשָׁ בַּת

5 שַׁבַּשׁ תָּשַׁב תַּבָּשׁ תַּבַּת בַּשָׁת

6 שַׁבַּב בַּתָּב תָּתַב בַּבָּת תַּבַּת

7 תַּבָּת שַׁבַּתָּ בַּשָׁת בַּשָׁשׁ בַּבָּת

8 שַׁבָּת שַׁבָּת שַׁבָּת שַׁבָּת שַׁבָּת

Heritage Word

Can you find this Hebrew word above? Read and circle it.

Shabbat שַׁבָּת

Challenge

God created the world in six days. On the seventh day God rested. Which line contains the name of that special day? 8

7

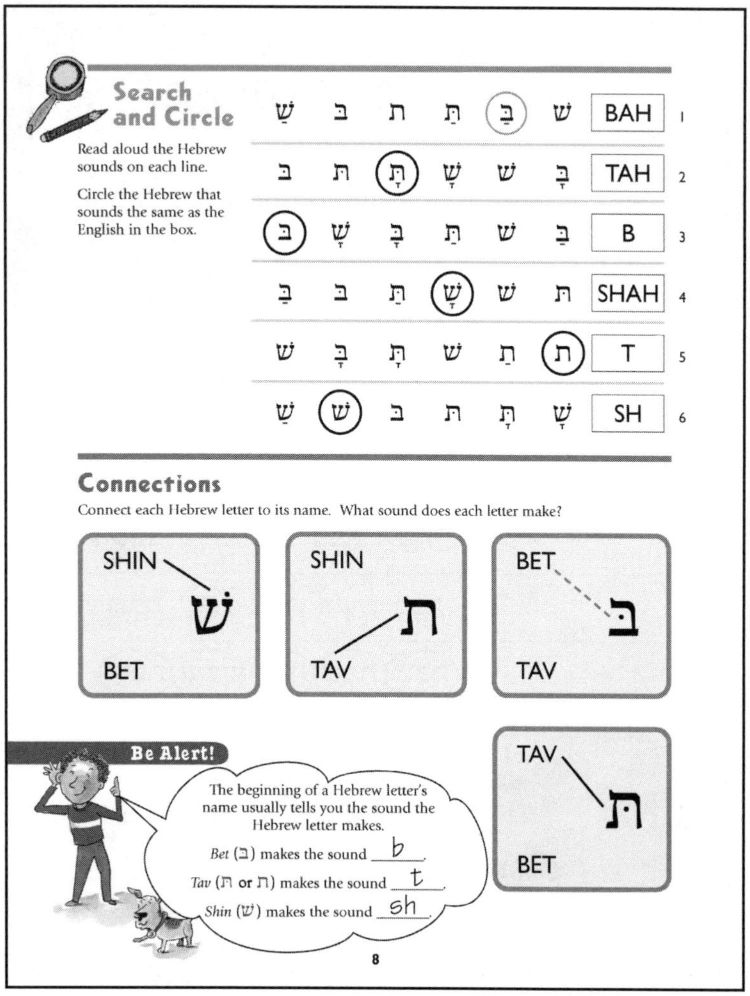
Search and Circle

Read aloud the Hebrew sounds on each line.

Circle the Hebrew that sounds the same as the English in the box.

שַׁ	ב	ת	תַּ	(בַּ)	שׁ	BAH	1
ב	ת	(תָּ)	שָׁ	שׁ	בָּ	TAH	2
(ב)	שָׁ	בָּ	תַּ	שׁ	בַּ	B	3
בַּ	ב	תַּ	(שָׁ)	שׁ	ת	SHAH	4
שׁ	בָּ	תָּ	שׁ	תַ	(ת)	T	5
שַׁ	(שׁ)	ב	ת	תָּ	שָׁ	SH	6

Connections

Connect each Hebrew letter to its name. What sound does each letter make?

SHIN / BET: שׁ	SHIN / TAV: ת	BET / TAV: בּ	TAV / BET: תּ

Be Alert!

The beginning of a Hebrew letter's name usually tells you the sound the Hebrew letter makes.

Bet (ב) makes the sound b.

Tav (ת or תּ) makes the sound t.

Shin (שׁ) makes the sound sh.

8

SEARCH AND CIRCLE/CONNECTIONS

Read the instructions and have the students complete these two exercises independently. Then have each pair up with a classmate to review their answers together.

If the students need additional practice in letter recognition, ask them to name all the letters in each row of the "Search and Circle" exercise.

PICTURE IT IN HEBREW

Say the new word—בַּיִת—several times to the class. Ask students to repeat the word while pointing to the house in the photograph. Call on individual students to say the Hebrew word for "house." Have students find and circle the new letter—בּ—in the word above the photograph. Then complete the activity together. Be sure to lead the reading of the new Hebrew word!

WELCOMING שַׁבָּת

After the students have completed the exercise independently, ask them to name each of the objects in the exercise that we use to welcome Shabbat. **[*ḥallah*, wine cup, candlesticks]**

Also review the other objects not related to Shabbat and identify when they are used. **[*gragger* on Purim, *lulav* and *etrog* on Sukkot]**

Ask the students what they can do on Shabbat to make it a special day.

If there is time, discuss with the students why they think God commanded us to have a day of rest. **[God rested on the seventh day of creation; we all need rest so we can spend time with our family and friends; so we can appreciate our Jewishness; so we can enjoy the world that God created.]**

ONLINE WORKBOOK

Assign activities from the *Shalom Uvrachah Primer Express Online Workbook* for review and reinforcement at home.
Visit www.behrmanhouse.com/suexpress to learn more.

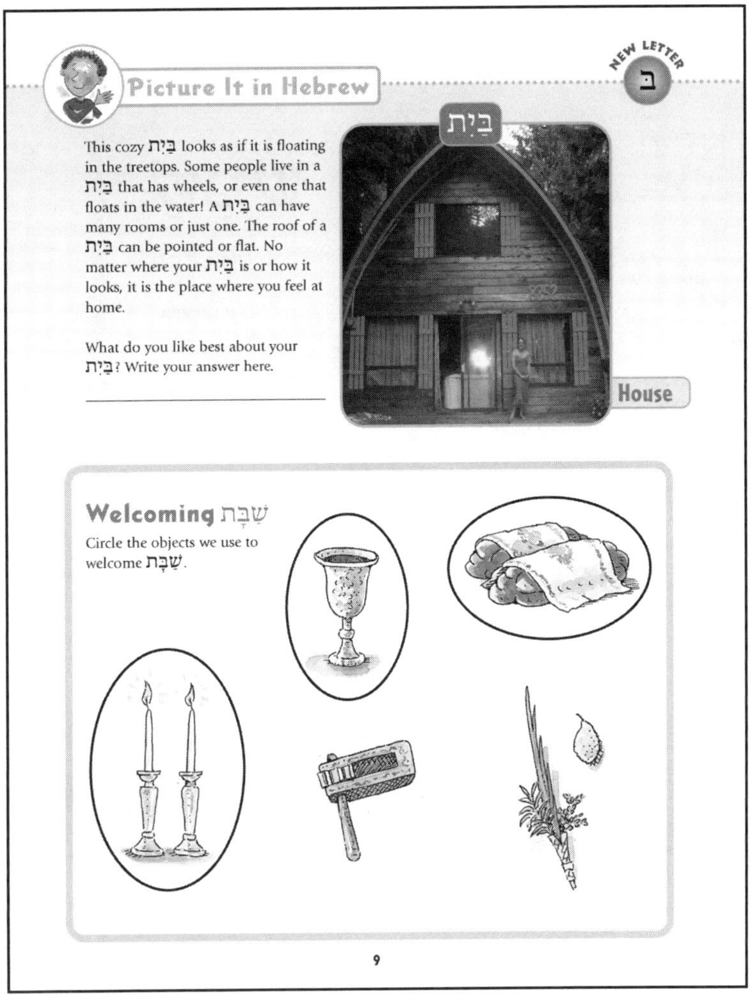

NEW LETTER בּ

Picture It in Hebrew

בַּיִת

This cozy בַּיִת looks as if it is floating in the treetops. Some people live in a בַּיִת that has wheels, or even one that floats in the water! A בַּיִת can have many rooms or just one. The roof of a בַּיִת can be pointed or flat. No matter where your בַּיִת is or how it looks, it is the place where you feel at home.

What do you like best about your בַּיִת? Write your answer here.

House

Welcoming שַׁבָּת

Circle the objects we use to welcome שַׁבָּת.

9

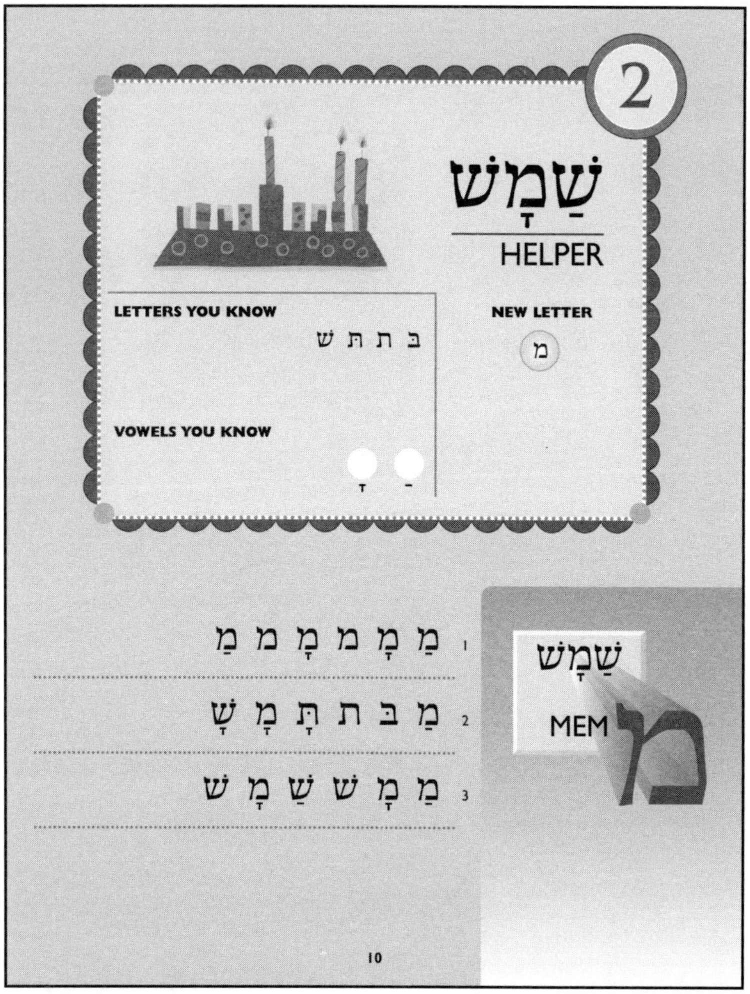

READING PRACTICE

Read line 1 for the class and have the students repeat the line in unison. Call on a student to read line 2 and then have the entire class repeat in unison. Repeat this procedure with line 3.

LESSON 2

Pages: 10–12
Key Word: שַׁמָּשׁ
New Letter: מ
Alef-Bet Flashcard: 7
Word Card: 3

KEY WORD (שַׁמָּשׁ)

Draw a picture of a Ḥanukkah *menorah* on the chalkboard or bring one in to show to the class. Point to the candleholder that is higher up or otherwise differentiated from the others.

- What is this candle called? **[*shamash*]**
- What is the job of the *shamash*? **[to light the other candles]**
- How many other candles are there? **[8]**
- What other times do we use candles in Judaism? **[welcome Shabbat and holidays; part of *Havdalah* ceremony to conclude Shabbat; *yahrtzeit* candle lit on anniversary of the death of a loved one]**
- Are there any other occasions when we use a *shamash*? **[no]**

INTRODUCING THE NEW LETTER – מ

Display word card #3 (שַׁמָּשׁ) or write the word on the chalkboard and have the students identify the vowels and letters they have already learned. **[ָ◌ ַ◌ שׁ]** Point to the letter *mem* and teach its name and sound.

Take *alef-bet* flashcards #1–7 and hold them facing you. Turn around one card per student and have each student take a turn identifying the name and sound of the letter or vowel. After you have gone through the seven cards, shuffle them and repeat, so each child will have a turn with a new letter or vowel.

Display word card #3 again and have the students read the complete word.

NOW READ & READ AGAIN

Call out a specific word, such as "line 3, fourth word" or "line 5, third word" and have a student read that word. Have the student call out the next word, or continue to call them out yourself.

HERITAGE WORD

Many synagogues used to have a person who was responsible for overseeing all the logistics of running the prayer services in the synagogue. This helper was called the *shamas*. The word *shamas* actually comes from the Yiddish language but it has the same root as the word *shamash*.

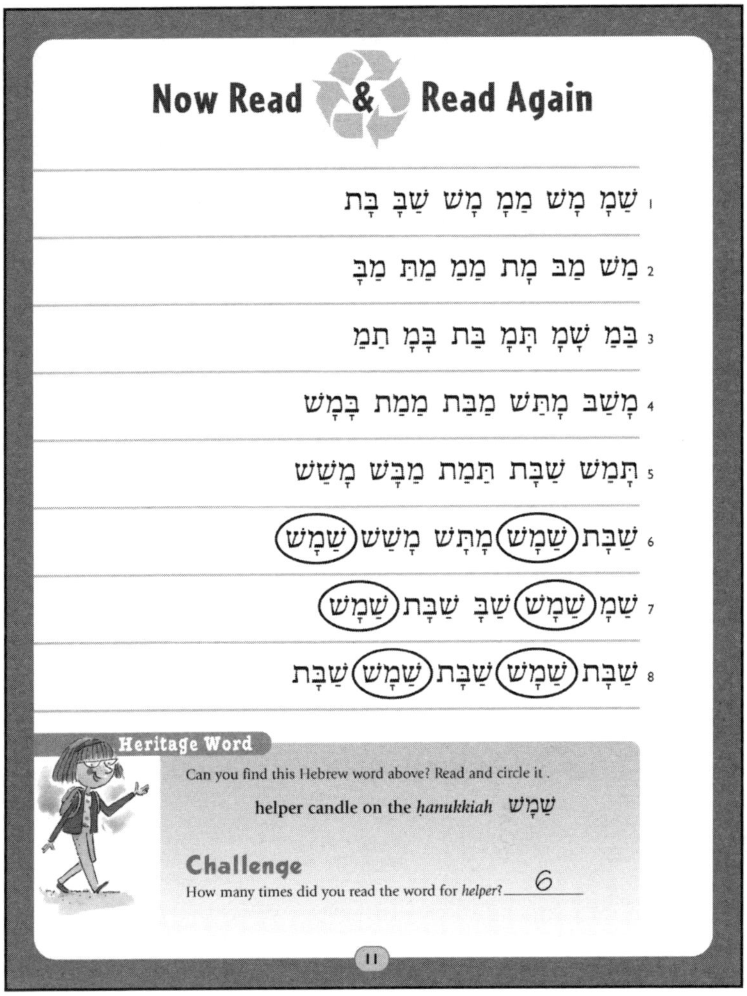

Now Read & Read Again

1 שַׁמָ מָשׁ מַמָ מָשׁ שַׁבָ בָּת

2 מַשׁ מַב מָת מַמַ מַתַּ מַבָּ

3 בַּמַ שָׁמָ תָּמָ בַּת בָּמָ תַמַ

4 מָשַׁב מָתַּשׁ מַבַּת מַמַת בָּמָשׁ

5 תָּמַשׁ שַׁבָּת תַּמַת מַבָּשׁ מָשַׁשׁ

6 שַׁבָּת שַׁמָשׁ מָתָּשׁ מָשַׁשׁ שַׁמָשׁ

7 שַׁמָ שַׁמָשׁ שַׁבָ שַׁבָּת שַׁמָשׁ

8 שַׁבָּת שַׁמָשׁ שַׁבָּת שַׁמָשׁ שַׁבָּת

Heritage Word

Can you find this Hebrew word above? Read and circle it.

helper candle on the *ḥanukkiah* שַׁמָשׁ

Challenge

How many times did you read the word for *helper*? 6

11

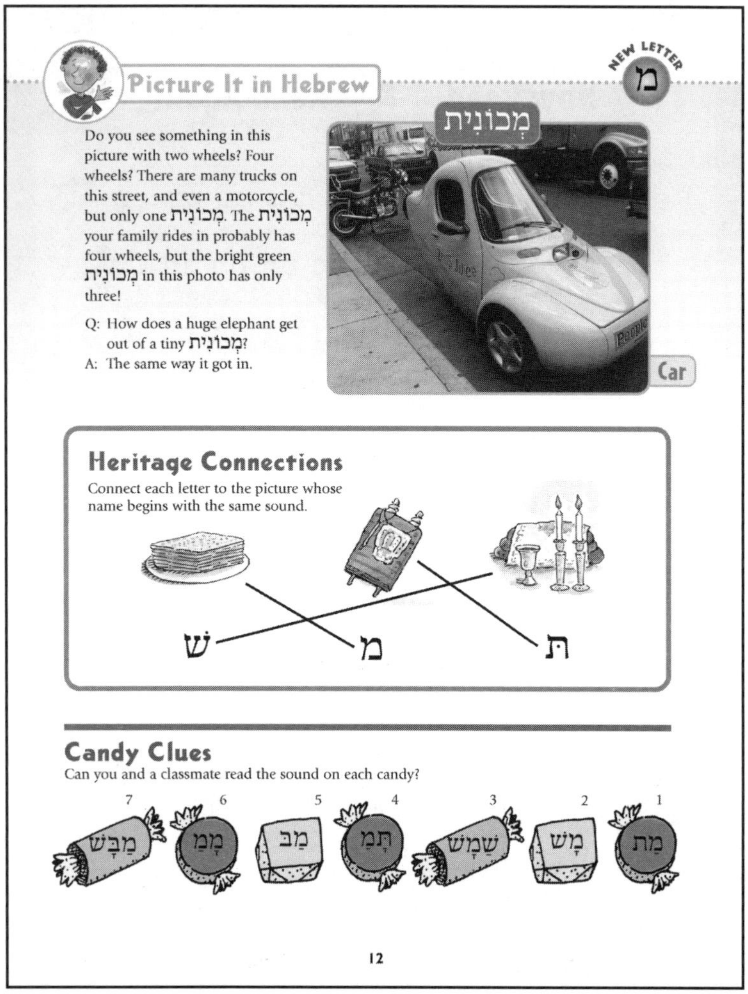

Picture It in Hebrew

NEW LETTER מ

מְכוֹנִית

Do you see something in this picture with two wheels? Four wheels? There are many trucks on this street, and even a motorcycle, but only one מְכוֹנִית. The מְכוֹנִית your family rides in probably has four wheels, but the bright green מְכוֹנִית in this photo has only three!

Q: How does a huge elephant get out of a tiny מְכוֹנִית?
A: The same way it got in.

Car

Heritage Connections

Connect each letter to the picture whose name begins with the same sound.

שׁ מ ת

Candy Clues

Can you and a classmate read the sound on each candy?

1 מַת 2 מָשׁ 3 שַׁמָשׁ 4 תָמַ 5 מַב 6 מָמַ 7 מַבָשׁ

12

ONLINE WORKBOOK

For fun homework that kids will want to do, Visit www.behrmanhouse.com/suexpress.

PICTURE IT IN HEBREW

Say the new word—מְכוֹנִית—several times to the class. Call on individual students to repeat the word. Have students find and circle the new letter—מ—in the word above the photograph. Call on several students to give its name and sound. **[*mem*, m]** Have students circle the word מְכוֹנִית every time it appears on the page. How many words did they circle? **[5]** Then complete the activity together.

For Review: Ask students the name and sound of the last letter in the word מְכוֹנִית. **[*tav*, t]**

HERITAGE CONNECTIONS

After students have completed the exercise independently, review the answers together aloud.

Go around the room and have the students quickly relate a happy memory connected with one of the pictures.

Another option is to divide the class into small groups and have them make up a short story that would include the words matzah, Torah, and Shabbat.

CANDY CLUES

For reading practice that is varied and fun, use the following techniques:

1. *As a class:* Play "What's Missing?" Have a student read the sounds on all the candies, omitting one. Call on another student to read the sound that the first student left out, and then to take a turn reading the sounds and omitting one. Continue until everyone has had a turn.
2. *In pairs:* Match stronger readers with weaker readers. Have students alternate with their partners, reading the sounds on the candy pieces, until both students in every pair have read each sound three times. See how quickly they can alternate reading the sounds.

LESSON 3

Pages: 13–17
Key Word: כַּלָּה
New Letters: ל כּ ה
Alef-Bet Flashcards: 8, 9, 10
Word Cards: 4, 5

REVIEW EXERCISE

In this lesson your class will learn three new letters. Therefore, it is essential the students have a firm grasp of the letters and vowels that they already know.

Review the letters and vowels from the last two lessons by using a flannelboard or chalkboard. Set up the board with the letters. Point to each in turn as the students call out the sound. Have them respond first in unison and then individually.

KEY WORD (כַּלָּה)

Have the students identify the picture at the top of the page. **[bride]**

Has anyone in the class attended a wedding? What was it like?

What things are unique to a Jewish wedding? **[*ḥuppah* – wedding canopy, *ketubah* – Jewish marriage contract, breaking the glass]**

Write the Key word – כַּלָּה – on the chalkboard or display word card #4 and read the word to the class. Explain that all three letters that make up this word will be taught during this lesson.

INTRODUCING THE NEW LETTER – ל

Introduce the new letter, *lamed*, by pointing it out in the word כַּלָּה. Write a *lamed* on the chalkboard. Write a vowel under the *lamed* and have each student take a turn sounding out the new letter/vowel combination. Alternate the vowels.

READING PRACTICE

Read the first line to the students and have them repeat the sounds in unison. Call on students to read line 2 and then have the class repeat in unison. Follow the same procedure for line 3.

Sounds Like

Read each line aloud.

Circle the Hebrew sounds on each line that are the same.

1	(מַשׁ)	שַׁמ	מָשׁ	(מַשׁ)
2	לָשׁ	(שָׁל)	(שַׁל)	שַׁל
3	בַּת	(בַּת)	(בָּת)	תַּב
4	(לַב)	בַּל	לַב	(לַב)
5	לַל	(לַמ)	(לָמ)	מַל

Search and Circle

Read aloud the Hebrew sounds on each line.

Circle the Hebrew that sounds the same as the English in the box.

1	LAH	ל	תַ	שׁ	(לָ)	בַ
2	M	מָ	(מ)	ת	ב	ל
3	MAH	שׁ	בַ	(מַ)	תָ	מ
4	L	(ל)	שׁ	ב	לָ	ת
5	SHAH	(שָׁ)	בַ	שׁ	ב	מַ

1 כַּ כָּ כ כַּ כָּ כ

2 כַּ בָּ ל תַ שָׁ מ

3 בָּ כַּ ת בָּ כָּ מַ

כַּלָּה

KAF

14

SOUNDS LIKE

Read aloud the sounds on each line while the students complete the exercise according to the instructions.

SEARCH AND CIRCLE

Have students complete the activity, then check a classmate's work.

INTRODUCING THE NEW LETTER – כּ

Display *alef-bet* flashcard #1 (בּ), or write it on the chalkboard, and have the class identify its name and sound. Then display *alef-bet* flashcard #9 (כּ) and teach its name and sound. How do these two letters differ in appearance?

Have the students point to the *kaf* in the Key word in their textbooks.

READING PRACTICE

Read the first line to the students and have them repeat the sounds in unison. Call on students to read line 2 or 3, allowing each student the opportunity to choose the line. Have them identify the line number before reading.

SOUND OFF

Have the students complete the exercise independently, and then call on individual students to say the name of the Hebrew letter and its sound.

INTRODUCE THE NEW LETTER – ה

Point to the *hay* on the *alef-bet* chart and teach its name and sound. Make sure to read and explain the "Be Alert" section.

READING PRACTICE

Have the students look at the Key word כַּלָּה and identify the name and sound of each letter. Have the students read the Key word and define it.

- Does the *hay* have the "h" sound in this word? **[no]**
- Why not? **[It is the final letter in the word and it has no vowel connected to it]**

Call on students at random to read one of the three lines.

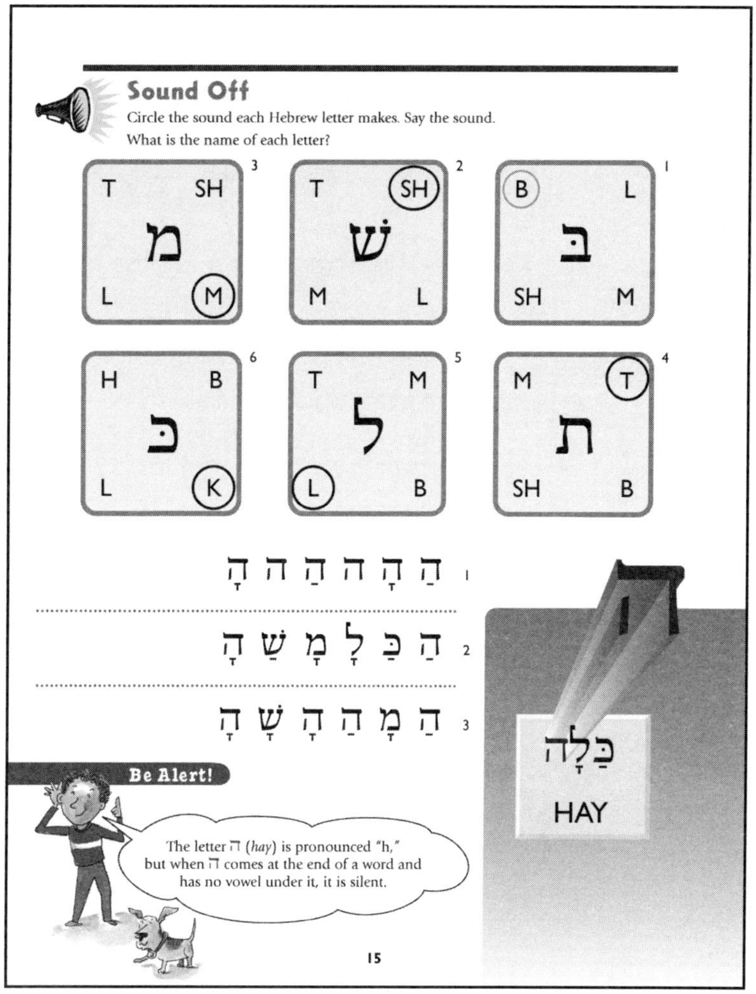
Sound Off

Circle the sound each Hebrew letter makes. Say the sound. What is the name of each letter?

1 בּ — B L SH M
2 שׁ — T SH M L
3 מ — T SH L M
4 ת — M T SH B
5 ל — T M L B
6 כּ — H B L K

1 הַ הָ ה הַ ה הָ

2 הַ כַּ לָ מָ שַׁ הָ

3 הַ מָ הַ הָ שָׁ הָ

כַּלָּה

HAY

Be Alert!

15

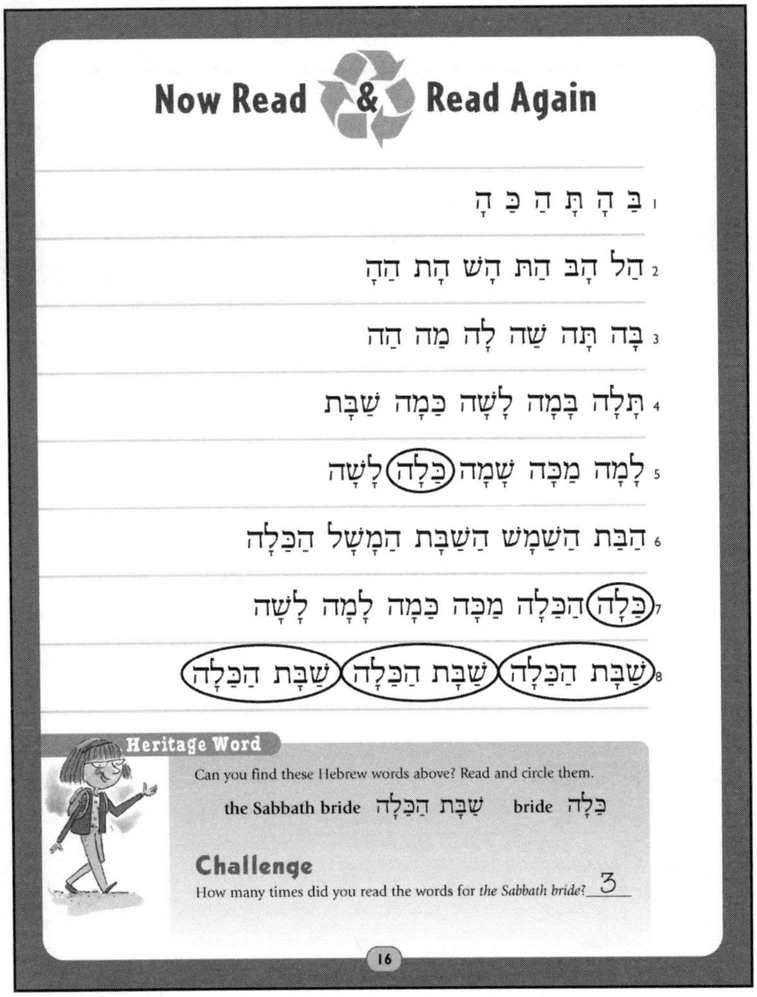

Now Read & Read Again

1 בַּ הָ תָּ הַ כַּ הָ

2 הַל הָב הַת הָשׁ הָת הַהָ

3 בָּה תָּה שַׁה לָה מַה הַה

4 תָּלָה בָּמָה לָשָׁה כַּמָה שַׁבָּת

5 לָמָה מַכָּה שָׁמָה כַּלָה לָשָׁה

6 הַבַּת הַשַּׁמָשׁ הַשַּׁבָּת הַמָשָׁל הַכַּלָה

7 כַּלָה הַכַּלָה מַכָּה כַּמָה לָמָה לָשָׁה

8 שַׁבָּת הַכַּלָה שַׁבָּת הַכַּלָה שַׁבָּת הַכַּלָה

Heritage Word

Can you find these Hebrew words above? Read and circle them.

the Sabbath bride שַׁבָּת הַכַּלָה   bride כַּלָה

Challenge

How many times did you read the words for *the Sabbath bride*? 3

16

NOW READ & READ AGAIN

Have students read three words at a time. The first student reads three words. The second student overlaps by reading three words beginning with the second word. The third student begins with the third word, and so on.

HERITAGE WORDS

At Shabbat services on Friday night we sing *L'cha Dodi Likrat Kallah.* Does anyone recognize this song? Can anyone sing the song or hum the tune?

This song compares Shabbat to a bride, and when we sing it we welcome the Shabbat bride.

- What words can be used to describe a bride on her wedding day? **[happy, glowing, nervous, excited, beautiful, etc.]**

PICTURE IT IN HEBREW

Ask: Who would wear the hats shown in the photograph? **[Israeli soldiers]**

Say the new word—כּוֹבַע—several times. Call on individual students to repeat the word. Complete the activity together. Then ask students to identify the middle letter of the word on the hats and to say its sound. **[*bay*, h]**

STEP BY STEP

Have students connect the dotted lines to complete the footprints. Assign the eight words on the footprints to eight different students. Have each student stand and take a step forward while reading the assigned word.

ONLINE WORKBOOK

To extend your classroom time, assign activities from the *Shalom Uvrachah Primer Express Online Workbook*.
Visit www.behrmanhouse.com/suexpress for more information.

Picture It in Hebrew

NEW LETTER בּ

When you visit Israel, you can buy a כּוֹבַע as a souvenir of the Israeli army. The Hebrew letters on each כּוֹבַע in this photograph—צ.ה.ל.—stand for the Hebrew words meaning "Israel Defense Forces."

How many times can you find the Hebrew letters for "Israel Defense Forces" in the photograph?

Write your answer here. 2

Word Match

Draw a line to match each Hebrew term with its English meaning. Read each Hebrew-English match aloud.

bride	שַׁבָּת
Sabbath	שַׁמָּשׁ
helper	שַׁבָּת הַכַּלָּה
the Sabbath bride	כַּלָּה

Step by Step

Connect the dashes to complete each footprint. Read each word as you "walk."

1 כַּלָּה
2 בַּת
3 שַׁבָּת
4 שַׁמָּשׁ
5 כַּלַּת
6 הַכַּלָּה
7 לָמָּה
8 בַּלַּת

17

READING PRACTICE

Randomly call on students to read each of these three lines. Remember, these lines can be repeated to give more students a chance to read.

LESSON 4

Pages: 18–21
Key Word: בְּרָכָה
New Letters: ר כ
New Vowel: ◌ְ
Alef-Bet Flashcards: 11, 12, 13
Word Card: 6

REVIEW EXERCISE

I Spy

Play the "I Spy" game described in #7 on page vii. Use flashcards #1–10.

This game can be modified by writing the letters and vowels on the chalkboard.

KEY WORD (בְּרָכָה)

What is the first word in almost every blessing we recite? **[*baruch*]** What is the Hebrew word for blessing? **[בְּרָכָה]**

Have the students list different *brachot* that they are familiar with. They will probably be surprised at how many they already know!

Have the students look at the Key word in the textbook and ask them to identify the names and sounds of the letters and vowels that they know. **[*bet*, *hay*, and *kamatz* – ◌ָ]**

INTRODUCING THE NEW LETTER – ר

Announce "I spy a *resh*!" and point to the *resh* on the *alef-bet* chart. Ask the students to guess the sound that the *resh* makes.

INTRODUCING THE NEW VOWEL – (*SHVAH*: ◌ְ)

Write a *shvah* on the chalkboard and ask if any of the students can "spy" it on the *alef-bet* chart. Take flashcards #5, 6, and 13 (the three vowels learned to this point) and drill the students on the vowel sounds.

NAME TAG

Have the students complete the exercise independently. When you are reviewing the answers together, after a student gives the correct answer have the student get up and "tag" a classmate to answer the next line.

INTRODUCE THE NEW LETTER – כ

Display *alef-bet* flashcard # 9 (כּ) and have the students identify its name and the sound it makes. Hold *alef-bet* flashcard #12 (כ) next to it and ask the students how the two differ in appearance. Teach the name and sound of the *chaf.* This can also be done by displaying these letters on a flannelboard.

The "*ch*" sound may be difficult for some students since there is no equivalent sound in English. You may want to compare it to the expression some people make regarding a food or something else which disgusts them – "*yuch.*" Be diligent in encouraging the students to pronounce the "*ch*" sound since some will lazily pronounce it "*k.*"

READING PRACTICE

Read line 1 for the class and have the class repeat the line in unison. Call on a student to read line 2 and then have the entire class repeat in unison. Repeat this procedure with line 3.

Have the students read the Key word – בְּרָכָה.

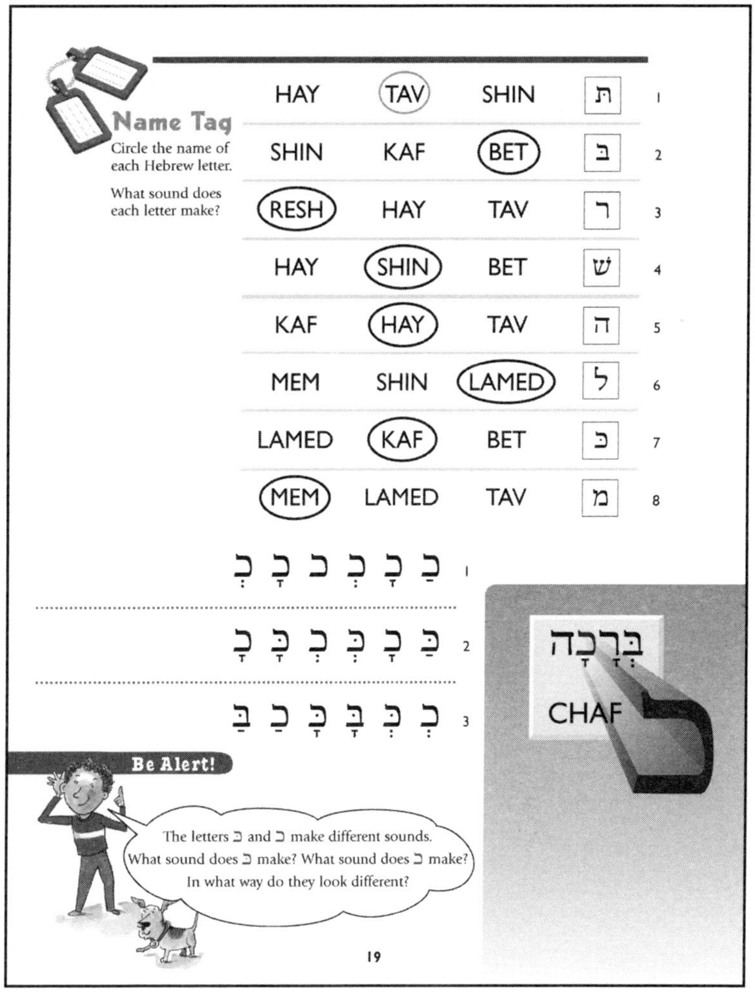

Name Tag

Circle the name of each Hebrew letter.

What sound does each letter make?

HAY	(TAV)	SHIN	ת	1
SHIN	KAF	(BET)	בּ	2
(RESH)	HAY	TAV	ר	3
HAY	(SHIN)	BET	שׁ	4
KAF	(HAY)	TAV	ה	5
MEM	SHIN	(LAMED)	ל	6
LAMED	(KAF)	BET	כּ	7
(MEM)	LAMED	TAV	מ	8

כַ כָ כְ כ כָ כְ 1

כַּ כָ כְּ כְ כָּ כָ 2

כְ כְּ בָּ כָּ כַ בַּ 3

בְּרָכָה

CHAF

Be Alert!

The letters כּ and כ make different sounds. What sound does כּ make? What sound does כ make? In what way do they look different?

19

Now Read & Read Again

1 מָכַ בָּכָ כָּכָ רָכַ תָּכָ לְכָ

2 כָּה מָכַ כָּכָ כַּבָּ כַּת כַשְׁ

3 רַכְ כָּמְ שַׁכְ כַּר תַּכַ בַּר

4 בָּכָה כָּכָה רַכָּה מָכַר שָׁכַר כַּלַת

5 כַּלָה כָּהָה כַּמָה מַכָּה רָכַשׁ לַכַּת

6 בָּכַת כָּכַת כָּרָה לְכָה תָּכָה לָכַשׁ

7 בָּכְתָה הַתָּכָה כָּרַכְתָּ מָכְרָה הָלַכְתָּ

8 הָלַכְתָּ בְּרָכָה בְּרָכָה הָלְכָה מָשְׁכָה

Heritage Word

Can you find this Hebrew word above? Read and circle it.

blessing בְּרָכָה

Challenge

How many times did you read the word for *blessing*? 2

20

NOW READ & READ AGAIN

Have a student read until you clap your hands. At that time, the next student reads. Determine the number of words according to the student's ability and reading fluency, keeping the pace lively. Students who can read faster may read more words and slower students may read fewer words in this exercise. Don't forget to recycle the reading exercise.

PICTURE IT IN HEBREW

Point to your head and say רֹאשׁ. Point to the heads of individual students and say רֹאשׁ. Then have students point to their own heads and say רֹאשׁ. Have students circle every occurrence of the word רֹאשׁ in the activity. How many words did they circle? **[10]** Read the paragraphs aloud to the class.

For Review: Ask students the name and sound of the last letter in the word רֹאשׁ. **[*shin*, sh]**

FRUIT OF THE TREE

Note: Write the words "daughter" and "queen" on the chalkboard to help students complete the exercise.

After the students are done, play "Fruit for Thought." Pass a paper plate with apple slices or dried apple pieces from student to student. Before students take a piece of fruit, they should say their "Challenge" sentence. Remember to recite the *brachah* before enjoying the snack.

ONLINE WORKBOOK

Assign activities from the online workbook and track your students' progress.

Picture It in Hebrew

NEW LETTER ר

רֹאשׁ means "head," but רֹאשׁ has other meanings as well. רֹאשׁ means "beginning," like רֹאשׁ הַשָּׁנָה—the beginning of the year. רֹאשׁ can also mean "leader," so in Israel, the Prime Minister is called רֹאשׁ הַמֶּמְשָׁלָה, the leader of the government. רֹאשׁ means "top," too.

In the photograph, the younger boy is knocking on the רֹאשׁ (top) of the older boy's רֹאשׁ (head)!

Fruit of the Tree

Read the Hebrew word on each apple. Then write the English meaning on the line above the apple.

Do you know the בְּרָכָה that we recite before we eat the fruit of the tree?

Challenge

Can you use each Hebrew word in an English sentence? Example: We welcome שַׁבָּת by lighting candles.

21

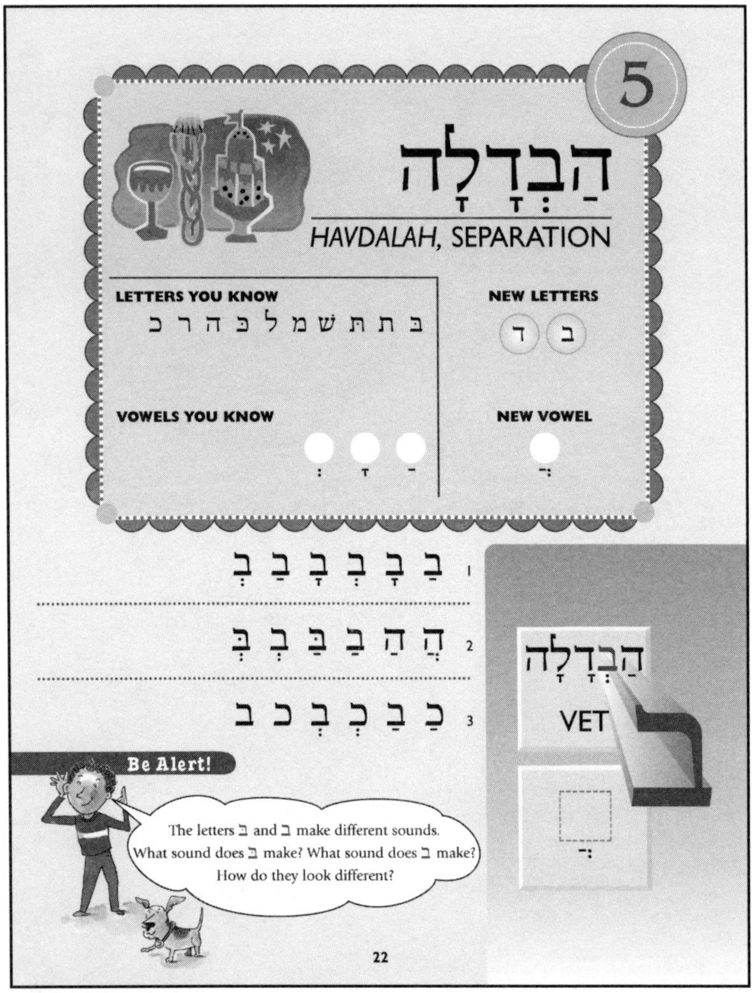

INTRODUCING THE NEW VOWEL – (*ḤATAF PATAḤ*: ◻ֲ)

Hold up flashcard #16 (◻ֲ). Ask the class what two vowels they recognize. Explain that this vowel is sounded the same as the *pataḥ*.

READING PRACTICE

Continuing the use of the "baseball theme," call on individuals to read each of the three lines and then have their teammates repeat in unison.

LESSON 5

Pages: 22–26
Key Word: הַבְדָלָה
New Letters: ד ב
New Vowel: ◻ֲ
Alef-Bet Flashcards: 14, 15, 16
Word Card: 9

REVIEW EXERCISE

Baseball

Play the "Baseball" game described in #5 on page v. Use flashcards #1–13.

Before the students tire of the game, take a "timeout" to introduce the new Key word, letter, and vowel. After the new letter and vowel are taught, return to the game, adding flashcards #14 and #16.

KEY WORD (הַבְדָלָה)

Display word card #1 (שַׁבָּת), or write the word on the chalkboard, and have the students read and define the word. Then ask the students to name the ceremony we recite on Saturday night at the end of Shabbat.

Explain that the word *havdalah* literally means "separation." Why do the students think we use *havdalah* as the name for this ceremony? **[It separates the holiness and specialness of Shabbat from the ordinary nature of the rest of the week.]** What objects do we use during the *havdalah* ceremony? **[spice box, Kiddush cup, braided candle]**

INTRODUCING THE NEW LETTER – ב

Have the students look at the Key word in the textbook or display word card #9. Which letters do they recognize? **[*hay, lamed*]** What does the second letter in the word resemble? **[*bet*]** How is it different? **[no dot]**
Hold up *alef-bet* flashcard #1 (בּ) next to flashcard #14 (ב). Pronounce clearly the difference in sounds.

WORD WIZARD

After the students have completed this exercise, write each of the Key words from the first four lessons on the chalkboard:

בְּרָכָה כַּלָּה שַׁמָּשׁ שַׁבָּת

Have the students define them, and then have the students choose one to embed in their own Word Wizard, as was done in the exercise with the word בְּרָכָה. Then have the students exchange their work and complete the exercise.

INTRODUCE THE NEW LETTER – ד

Point to the *resh* on the *alef-bet* chart and have the students identify its name and the sound it makes. Then point to the *dalet* and teach its name and sound. How do these two letters differ in appearance? A helpful hint to the students is always to remember that "*resh* is rounded."

Display word card #9 or write the Key word on the chalkboard, and have the students point out the *dalet* in the word and then read the word.

READING PRACTICE

As a change of pace, tell the students to read the sounds on the three lines vertically. This variation will provide six columns of three sounds each.

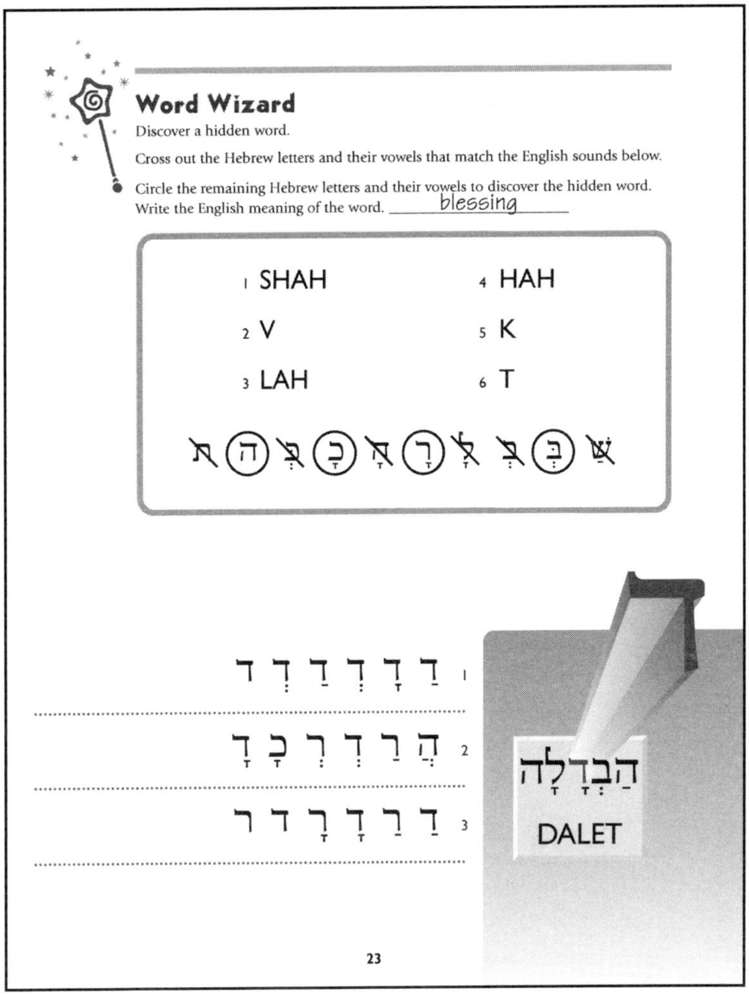

Word Wizard

Discover a hidden word.

Cross out the Hebrew letters and their vowels that match the English sounds below.

Circle the remaining Hebrew letters and their vowels to discover the hidden word.

Write the English meaning of the word. blessing

1 SHAH	4 HAH
2 V	5 K
3 LAH	6 T

שַׁ בְּ בְ לָ רָ הָ כָ בְ ה ת

1 דַ דָ דְ דַ דְ ד

2 הֲ רַ דְ רְ כָ דָ

3 דַ רַ דָ רָ ד ר

הַבְדָּלָה

DALET

23

Now Read & Read Again

1 דָד דָר בַּד בַּר דָשׁ רָשׁ

2 דָשׁ דַת דַל דָה דָר דָב

3 מַד כַּד בַּךָ שַׁךָ הַד רַד

4 דָלָה דָבָר דְבַשׁ לָמַד הָדָר דָרָה

5 לְבַד דָהָה דָרַשׁ שָׁדַד דָשָׁה מָדַד

6 הֲמָרָה דְמָמָה הֲלָכָה הֲדָרָה הֲבָרָה

7 כָּתְבָה לָבַשְׁתָּ לָמְדָה דָרַכְתָּ מָדְדָה

8 הַבְדָלָה דְרָשָׁה הֲלָכָה בְּרָכָה הַבְדָלָה

Heritage Word

Can you find this Hebrew word above? Read and circle it.

havdalah, separation הַבְדָלָה

Challenge

How many times did you read the word for *separation?* 2

24

NOW READ & READ AGAIN

Call on students at random to read each of the lines. Keep students on their toes by calling on the same child more than once.

HERITAGE WORD

An additional question to ask is, "What other words that you have learned appear above?" **[בְּרָכָה]** If the students cannot figure it out, give them the hint to look in line 8.

SOUNDS LIKE

Have the students complete this exercise independently, and then call on students to read each line and provide the answer.

GREEN THUMB

Cut out leaf shapes from construction paper. On each leaf, write one of the letters featured in this exercise. Make two leaves for each letter. Students who finish the activity early can play Concentration, in which they try to pair matching letters.

Challenge: Students must say the name of the letter before claiming a pair.

Sounds Like

Read the Hebrew sound in each box.

Read the Hebrew sounds on each line.

Circle the Hebrew sound on each line that is the same as the Hebrew in the box.

	Box			
1	הָבָ	תַב	(הַבַ)	הָרָ
2	בַּד	(בָּדְ)	בַּרְ	כַּד
3	רָשָׁה	דָשָׁה	רָתָה	(רָשַׁ)
4	כָּכְ	(כַּכְ)	בָּבְ	כַּבְ
5	דָבָר	דָבַה	רָבָד	(דַבַר)

Green Thumb

Color the leaf with the Hebrew letter that matches the name in the flower.

25

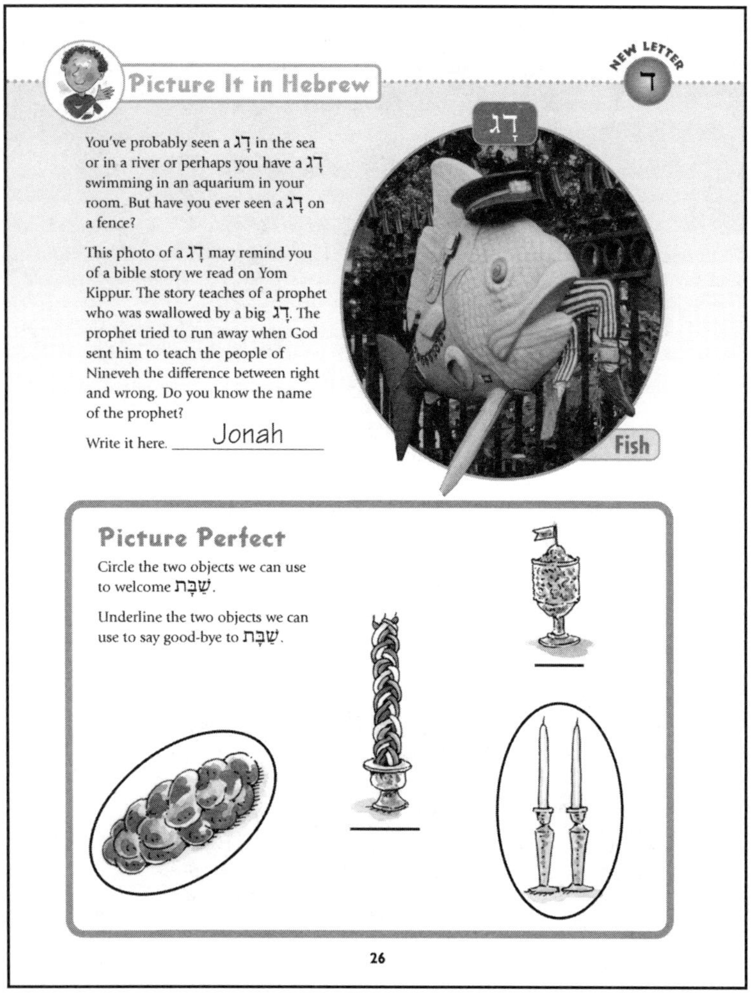

NEW LETTER ד

Picture It in Hebrew

דָג

You've probably seen a דָג in the sea or in a river or perhaps you have a דָג swimming in an aquarium in your room. But have you ever seen a דָג on a fence?

This photo of a דָג may remind you of a bible story we read on Yom Kippur. The story teaches of a prophet who was swallowed by a big דָג. The prophet tried to run away when God sent him to teach the people of Nineveh the difference between right and wrong. Do you know the name of the prophet?

Write it here. Jonah

Fish

Picture Perfect

Circle the two objects we can use to welcome שַׁבָּת.

Underline the two objects we can use to say good-bye to שַׁבָּת.

26

PICTURE IT IN HEBREW

Call on students to read the first letter and vowel in the word דָג. Read the word to them several times and have them repeat it. Then have students complete the activity.

Enrichment: Bring in a story about the prophet Jonah to read to the class or read the verses from the Book of Jonah in which Jonah is swallowed by "a great fish" (Jonah 2:1).

PICTURE PERFECT

Have students compare the drawings in "Picture Perfect" with the illustration on page 22. Ask them what object is missing from "Picture Perfect." **[the wine glass]** Ask: In addition to Havdalah, on what other occasions do we use this object? **[for Kiddush on Shabbat and holidays; at weddings]**

ONLINE WORKBOOK

Assign activities from the online workbook and track your students' progress.

LESSON 6

Pages: 27–30
Key Word: וְאָהַבְתָּ
New Letters: ו א
Alef-Bet Flashcards: 17, 18
Word Card: 10

REVIEW EXERCISE

Go Fish

Put *alef-bet* flashcards #1–17 into a bag and have each child take a turn fishing out a letter and giving its name and/or sound. One of the students will choose card #17 (א). After the students come to the conclusion that they don't recognize this letter, you can explain that this is the letter to be learned in this lesson. Have that student go to the *alef-bet* chart and point out the matching letter, and then put card #17 aside until all the other cards have been fished out of the bag.

KEY WORD (וְאָהַבְתָּ)

- Which prayer tells us to love God? **[first paragraph after the Shema – *Ve'ahavta*...]**
- Why does our tradition teach us to love God? **[God created the world; God cares for us, etc.]**

If your class is familiar with the tune sung to the Ve'ahavta paragraph, sing it at this time.

INTRODUCING THE NEW LETTER – א

Once again display *alef-bet* flashcard #17 and introduce the *alef* to the class. Be sure the students understand the idea of a letter that is not sounded. If the students have difficulty with this concept, you can teach the *alef* as a letter that takes the sound of the vowel connected to it. Have the students look at the Key word in the textbook and point to the *alef*.

READING PRACTICE

Call on a student to read line 1 for the class and have the class repeat the line in unison. Repeat this procedure with lines 2 and 3.

6

וְאָהַבְתָּ

AND YOU SHALL LOVE

LETTERS YOU KNOW

בּ ת תּ שׁ מ ל כּ ה ר כ ב ד

VOWELS YOU KNOW

ֲ ְ ָ ַ

NEW LETTERS

א ו

1 אַ אֲ אָ אֲ אָ אַ

2 אָ שָׁ לְ הֲ רָ בְּ

3 אֲ הָ אָ דָ כְּ רְ

וְאָהַבְתָּ

ALEF

27

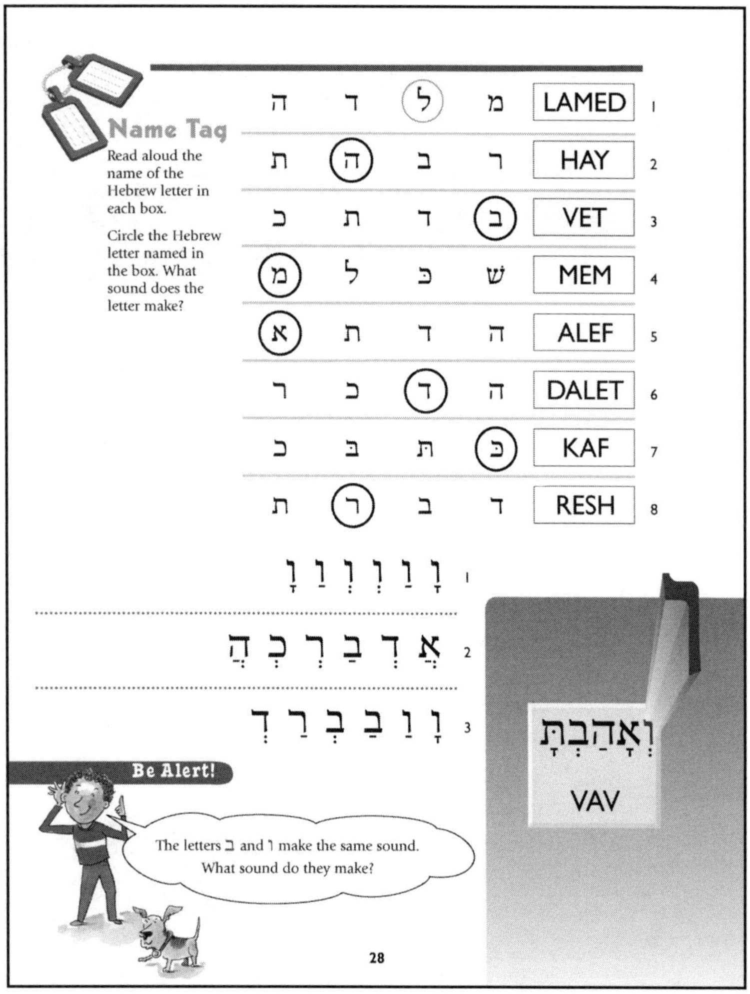

Name Tag

Read aloud the name of the Hebrew letter in each box.

Circle the Hebrew letter named in the box. What sound does the letter make?

ה	ד	(ל)	מ	LAMED	1
ת	(ה)	ב	ר	HAY	2
כ	ת	ד	(ב)	VET	3
(מ)	ל	כּ	ש	MEM	4
(א)	ת	ד	ה	ALEF	5
ר	כ	(ד)	ה	DALET	6
כ	בּ	תּ	(כּ)	KAF	7
ת	(ר)	ב	ד	RESH	8

1 וָ וַ וְ וְ וַ וָ

2 אֱ דְ בַ רְ כְ הֱ

3 וָ וַ בַ בְ רַ דְ

Be Alert!

The letters ב and ו make the same sound. What sound do they make?

וְאָהַבְתָּ

VAV

28

NAME TAG

Read aloud the name of the Hebrew letter in each box and ask the students to circle the matching Hebrew letter on that line.

INTRODUCING THE NEW LETTER – ו

Using the flannelboard or chalkboard, display the letters *resh*, *dalet*, and *vet*. Make each letter a different color, if possible. Have the students identify their names and the sound they make. Add the *vav* and teach its name and sound. What other letter has the same sound as the *vav*? **[*vet*]** How does the *vav* differ in appearance from the *resh* and *dalet*?

READING PRACTICE

Ask the students to look at the Key word in the textbook, read it, define it, and name each of the letters that comprise the word.

Call on a student to read line 1 for the class and have the class repeat the line in unison. Repeat this procedure with lines 2 and 3.

NOW READ & READ AGAIN

Call out a specific word, such as "line 3, fourth word" and have a student read that word. Have the student call out the next word, or continue to call out yourself.

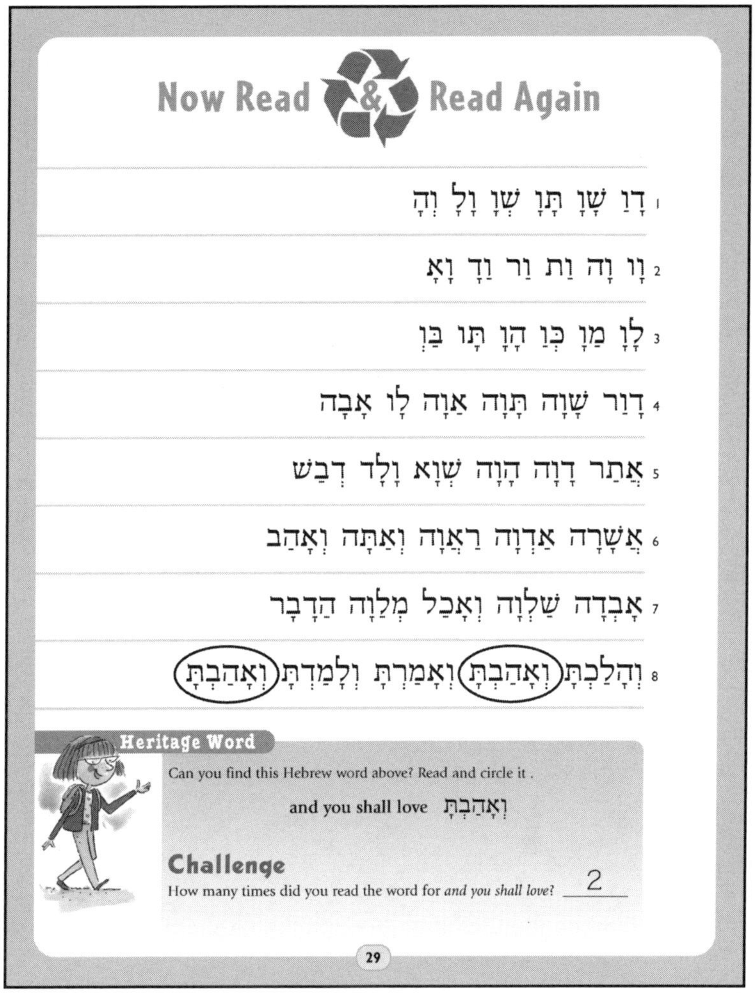

Now Read & Read Again

1 דָוַ שָׁו תָּו שְׁו וָל וְהָ

2 וָו וָה וַת וַר וַדָ וָאָ

3 לָוָ מַוָ כְּוַ הָוָ תָּו בַּוְ

4 דָוַר שָׁוָה תָּוָה אַוָה לָו אָבָה

5 אֲתַר דָוָה הָוָה שְׁוָא וָלָד דְבַשׁ

6 אֲשָׁרָה אַדְוָה רַאֲוָה וְאַתָּה וְאָהַב

7 אָבְדָה שַׁלְוָה וְאָכַל מְלַוָה הַדָּבָר

8 וְהָלַכְתָּ וְאָהַבְתָּ וְאָמַרְתָּ וְלָמַדְתָּ וְאָהַבְתָּ

Heritage Word

Can you find this Hebrew word above? Read and circle it.

and you shall love וְאָהַבְתָּ

Challenge

How many times did you read the word for *and you shall love*? 2

29

Picture It in Hebrew

NEW LETTER א

אָח, אָחוֹת

Do you have an אָח or אָחוֹת like the boy and girl in this photo? The אָח and אָחוֹת in this photograph look like each other, but sometimes an אָח and אָחוֹת might look completely different from each other. Your אָח or אָחוֹת may play with you, or argue with you, but one thing is for sure—your אָח or אָחוֹת will always care about you!

Brother, Sister

MIX AND MATCH

Draw a line to match each Hebrew term with its English meaning.

Read each Hebrew-English match aloud.

בְּרָכָה	Sabbath, rest	1
וְאָהַבְתָּ	blessing	2
שַׁבָּת	and you shall love	3

כַּלָּה	*havdalah*, separation	4
הַבְדָּלָה	helper	5
שַׁמָּשׁ	bride	6

30

PICTURE IT IN HEBREW/MIX AND MATCH

Ask students to look carefully at the "Mix and Match" activity at the bottom of the page and to find the Hebrew word containing the letter **א**. Tell them that the word describes the way an אָח and אָחוֹת usually feel about each other. Have students read the word aloud and give its English meaning.

Ask: Who in the class has an אָח or an אָחוֹת? Consider teaching students the following Hebrew expressions:

- "I have a brother"—יֵשׁ לִי אָח (*yesh li aḥ*).
- "I have a sister"—יֵשׁ לִי אָחוֹת (*yesh li aḥot*).
- "I have a brother and a sister"— יֵשׁ לִי אָח וְאָחוֹת (*yesh li aḥ v'aḥot*).

ONLINE WORKBOOK

Assign activities from the online workbook and track your students' progress.

LESSON 7

Pages: 31–34
Key Word: צְדָקָה
New Letters: צ ק
Alef-Bet Flashcards: 19, 20
Word Cards: 12, 14

REVIEW EXERCISE

Distribute *alef-bet* flashcards #1–18 randomly to students. Class size will determine how many cards each student receives.

Call out the name or sound of a letter or vowel and have the student with that card hold it up as it is called. Consider calling out letter/vowel combinations to add complexity to this exercise. For example, when calling the word *mar* the students with the *mem*, *resh*, *pataḥ*, *kamatz*, and *ḥataf pataḥ* cards should all display them.

KEY WORD (צְדָקָה)

Ask the students if they have ever heard of the Hebrew word *tsedakah*. What does it mean? **[justice]** Why is *tsedakah* important and what would the world be like if people did not perform acts of *tsedakah*?

Have the students think of causes that they would like to support (e.g., homelessness, muscular dystrophy, the environment) and have each one say and complete this sentence:

"If I had $1000, I would give it to _________ as *tsedakah*."

INTRODUCING THE NEW LETTER – ק

Point to the *koof* on the *alef-bet* chart and ask the student holding this letter to display it. Teach the letter *koof* and its sound. What letter already learned has the same sound? ***[kaf]*** Display word card #12 and point out the location of the *kuf*.

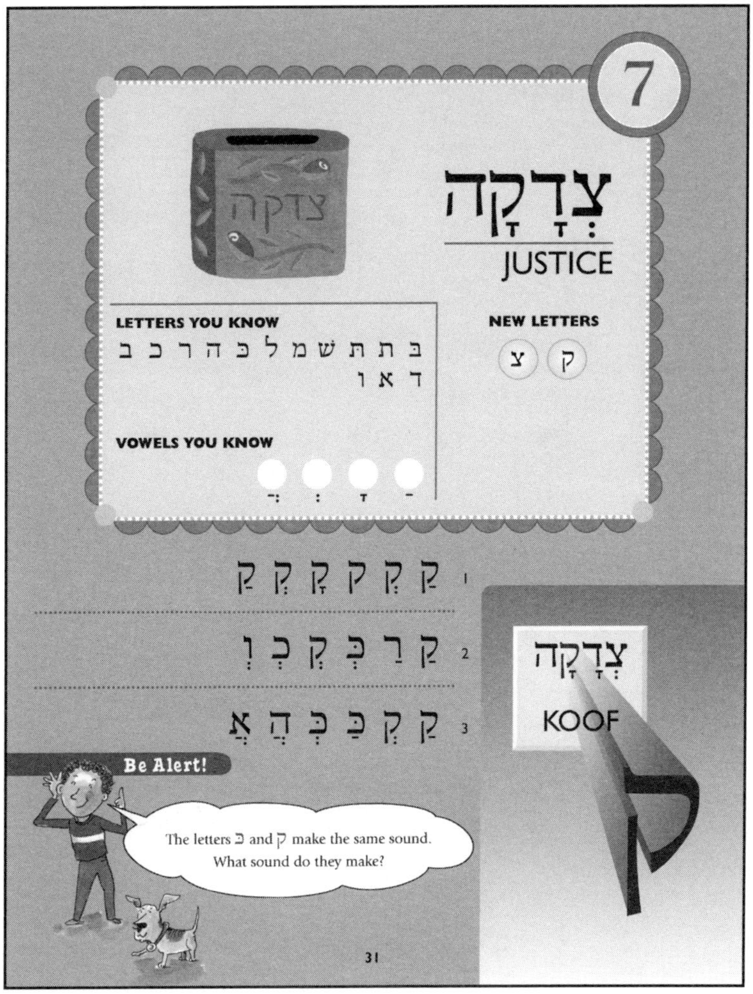

READING PRACTICE

Have the students open their books. Read the first line aloud to the class and have the students repeat the sounds in unison. Call on a student to read line 2 and then have the other students repeat in unison. Follow the same procedure for line 3.

Sound Off

Say the name of the Hebrew letter in each box.
Circle the English letter that makes the same sound as the Hebrew letter.

Hebrew letter	Choices (circled answer in parentheses)
מ	V, (M), R
ק	(K), CH, L
ה	(H), V, T
ל	T, (L), SH
ו	(V), H, M
ד	R, K, (D)

1 צַ צְ צָ צ צַ צְ

2 קַ צַ קְ כְּ צְ לְ

3 צַ צְ קַ קְ כְּ דְ

צְדָקָה
TSADEE

32

SOUND OFF

Have the students complete this exercise independently, and then review the answers together.

INTRODUCING THE NEW LETTER – צ

Display word card #12 (צְדָקָה) or look at the Key word in the book. Which letter in this word has not yet been learned? **[first letter]** Read the word slowly and ask what sound the first letter makes. **[ts]** Teach the name and review its sound. What English words have a similar sound in them? **[e.g., pizza, boats, etc.]**

READING PRACTICE

Read the first line and have the students respond in unison. Call on students to first read lines 2 or 3 and then repeat it singing the sounds to a simple tune such as "Twinkle Twinkle Little Star" or "Mary Had a Little Lamb."

NOW READ & READ AGAIN

Have one student read a line. Then that student calls out the next line number to be read.

HERITAGE WORDS

After completing the Heritage words exercise with the words צְדָקָה and מַצָּה, teach the class about the Jewish concept of *maot ḥittim* – מָעוֹת חִטִּים. **[special funds traditionally raised by the Jewish community before *Pesaḥ* for the purpose of providing *matzot* and other Passover needs for the poor]**

Now Read & Read Again

1 צַו צָב צַר צַד צָה צָל

2 כְּצַ בָּצַ אָצָ מַצָ קָצַ רָצָ

3 אָכָה צָדַק כְּצַד בָּצַר אָצָה צָרָה

4 צָבָא צָבַּר קָצַר צְבָת בָּצָל מָצָא

5 מַצָּה קְצַת קַצָב מַצָב הַצָב אָצַר

6 מָצָא צָלָה צָמַד מַצָּה אָצְתָ צָמָא

7 וְרָצָה וְאָצַר צָרַמְתְּ צָוָאר צָוְאָה

8 צְדָקָה בָּצַרְתָּ מָצָאתָ צָדַקְתָּ צְדָקָה

Heritage Words

Can you find these Hebrew words above? Read and circle them.

justice צְדָקָה matzah מַצָּה

Challenge

Each year at Passover we eat a special food in place of bread.

Do you recognize the name of the food?

33

NEW LETTER צ

Picture It in Hebrew

Do you belong to the Boy Scouts or Girl Scouts? In Israel, boys and girls participate together in all צוֹפִים activities. Students in every part of Israel join the צוֹפִים. The צוֹפִים have fun, and they help their communities, too. You may have seen the צוֹפִים Friendship Caravan, thirty students who are chosen each summer to visit North America, bringing the spirit of Israel to audiences through song and dance.

What symbol do you see on the צוֹפִים uniforms? Write your answer here. Israeli flag

Picture Perfect

Draw a line to connect each picture with its matching Hebrew word.

34

PICTURE IT IN HEBREW

Read the word צוֹפִים several times to the class. Point to the photo of the scouts and repeat the word.

Ask: What is the name of the first letter in the word? ***[tsadee]*** What sound does it make? **[ts]**

Choose one student to read the paragraph and another to say the word צוֹפִים each time it appears.

Call on a student to provide the answer to the question at the end.

PICTURE PERFECT

Have students complete the activity individually then check one another's work.

ONLINE WORKBOOK

Assign activities from the online workbook and track your students' progress.

LESSON 8

Pages: 35–37
Key Word: מִצְוָה
New Vowels: □ִ י□ִ
Alef-Bet Flashcards: 21, 22
Word Cards: 15, 16, 17, 18, 19, 20

KEY WORD (מִצְוָה)

Ask the students to define the word mitzvah. Have the students make a list of all the *mitzvot* performed in a day (e.g., studying, being respectful to parents and teachers, helping the needy, washing up in the morning, etc.).

INTRODUCING THE NEW VOWEL – (*HIRIK*: □ִ י□ִ)

Write the Key word (מִצְוָה) on the chalkboard. What letter or vowel in this word has not yet been learned? **[the vowel under the *mem*]** Pronounce the word מִצְוָה clearly and ask what sound they think this vowel makes. Then formally introduce this vowel and its sound.

Write on the chalkboard in random order all the vowels learned to this point. Point to each vowel and call on a student to pronounce its sound.

READING PRACTICE

Tell the class there was once a famous actress who was so talented that she was able to bring tears to the eyes of an audience simply by reciting the alphabet. Instruct the students to read the line of syllables dramatically, as if they were on stage. For example, suggest that the first person read the line angrily, the second person sadly, and so on.

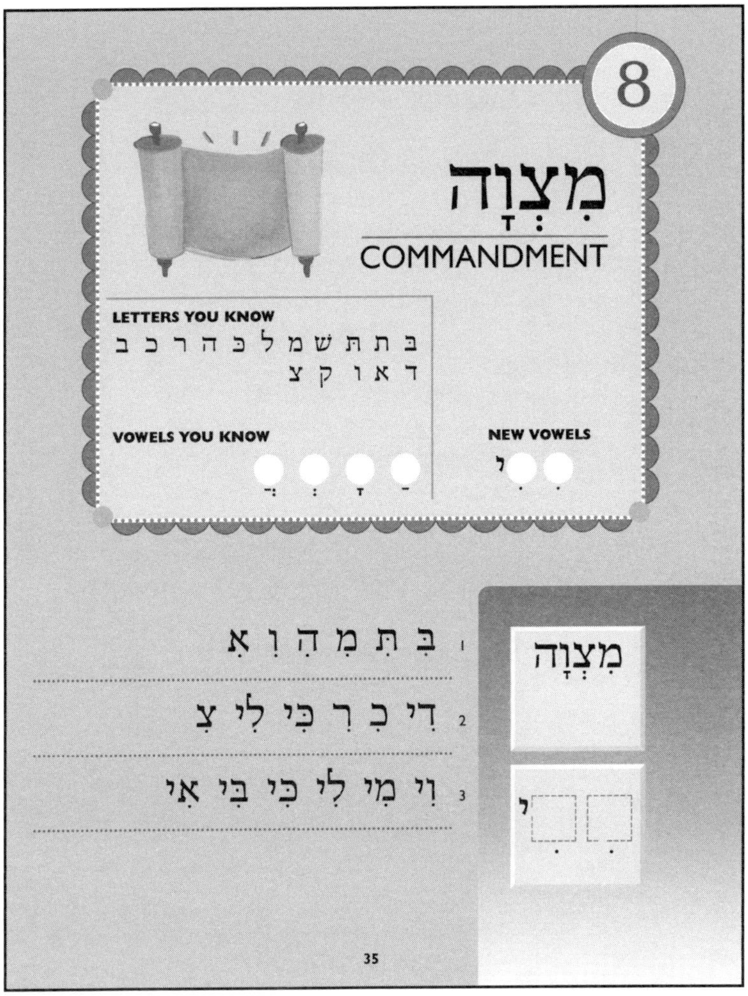
8

מִצְוָה

COMMANDMENT

LETTERS YOU KNOW

בּ ת תּ ש מ ל כּ ה ר כ ב

ד א ו ק צ

VOWELS YOU KNOW

NEW VOWELS

1 בִּ תִּ מִ הִ וִ אִ

2 דִי כִ רִ כִּי לִי צִ

3 וִי מִי לִי כִּי בִּי אִי

מִצְוָה

35

Now Read & Read Again

1 מִק צַדִי לְבִי אֱוִי דָו בְּרִי

2 שִׁשָׁה הִכָּה בִּיב שְׁמִי צִיר הֱכִי

3 הִיא אִיש אִשָּׁה אִמָא בְּכִי בְּלִי

4 רַבִּי אֲוִיר דָוִד בִּימָה דָתִי תִּיק

5 שִׁירָה תִּירָא רִמָה קְרִיאַת לְבִיבָה קָצִיר

6 צַדִיק בְּרִיאַת קַדִישׁ אָבִיב קְהִילָה מִקְרָא

7 צִיצִית בְּרִית מִילָה תִּקְוָה הַתִּקְוָה

8 מִצְוָה הַמִצְוָה בַּר מִצְוָה בַּת מִצְוָה

Heritage Word

Can you find these Hebrew words above? Read and circle them.

knotted fringes on the corners of the *tallit*	צִיצִית	commandment	מִצְוָה
Kaddish	קַדִישׁ	bar mitzvah	בַּר מִצְוָה
the Hope, the national anthem of Israel	הַתִּקְוָה	bat mitzvah	בַּת מִצְוָה

A בַּר מִצְוָה or בַּת מִצְוָה may wear a *tallit*. The *tallit* has knotted fringes on the four corners. Circle the Hebrew word for *knotted fringes* above.

36

NOW READ & READ AGAIN

Call on a student to read the first three words on line 1. Then call on another student to read the next three words until all the words have been read.

When recycling this exercise, ask the students to follow these instructions for each line:

Line #	Instructions
1)	Read the words that contain a *dalet*
2)	Read the words that begin with a *hay*
3)	Read the words that contain an *alef*
4)	Read the words that contain a *bet*
5)	Read the words that contain a *kamatz*
6)	Read the words that contain a *kuf*
7)	Read the words that contain a *ḥirik*
8)	Read the word that appears three times

HERITAGE WORDS

קַדִישׁ is the name of a prayer proclaiming God's holiness and uniqueness. There are several versions of the Kaddish, recited at different points during services. The best known version is the Mourner's Kaddish. Your students may be surprised to learn that the Mourner's Kaddish makes no mention of death. It is recited by those in mourning because they are declaring their faith in God despite the loss of their loved one.

Why do you think the national anthem of Israel is called הַתִּקְוָה – The Hope? **[The Jewish people have long hoped and prayed for the return to their own land.]**

After the students have completed the exercise, ask what the significance of the צִיצִית is. **[They remind us to do God's commandments, the *mitzvot*.]**

PICTURE IT IN HEBREW

The word מוּסִיקָה should be easy for students to understand since it sounds so similar to "music." (A word that is related to one in a different language is called a "cognate.") Say the word several times, and have students repeat it after you. Ask students the name and sound of the first letter in the word. **[*mem*, m]**

Ask students their favorite kinds of music, and have them fill in their answers on the blank line in the activity.

ONLINE WORKBOOK

Assign activities from the online workbook and track your students' progress.

NEW VOWEL

Picture It in Hebrew

מוּסִיקָה

You can listen to מוּסִיקָה almost anywhere. This musician is playing מוּסִיקָה on the street, but you can buy tapes or CDs from him and listen to מוּסִיקָה at home or in the car. מוּסִיקָה can wake you up or calm you down.

What is your favorite kind of מוּסִיקָה? Write your answer here.

____

Music

Search and Circle

Read each line aloud.
Find and circle the Hebrew letter that is found in every word on the line.
Say the name of the letter and its sound.

1 מַלְבִּישׁ רַבִּי מִדְבָּר דִּבְּרָה

2 אִרְא בְּקִרְבִּי פֵּרוֹת מִדְרָשׁ

3 תָּמִיד מִדָּה בָּמָה אָמַרְתִּי

4 מַצִּיל צְדָקָה צִיצִית מִצְוָה

5 הַתִּקְוָה אָבִיו צִוָּה בְּשַׁלְוֹ

6 לְהָבִיא אִשָּׁה אָהַבְתִּי קְהִלָּה

37

LESSON 9

Pages: 38–40
Key Word: שְׁמַע
New Letter: ע
Alef-Bet Flashcard: 23
Word Cards: 21, 22

REVIEW EXERCISE

Packing Grandmother's Suitcase

Play the "Grandmother's Suitcase" game described in #6 on page vii. Use *alef-bet* flashcards #1–22. If you are not teaching the names of the vowels, have the students say the vowel sounds.

KEY WORD (שְׁמַע)

Hold up word card #21 (שְׁמַע) and say, "I packed my grandmother's suitcase and in it I put the Shema." Do the students recognize this word? From where? What does it mean? **[hear]**

Sing the Shema together. How do you feel when you sing the Shema?

Why is the Shema one of the most important prayers in Judaism? **[It declares our belief and faith in our God, the only God. Some people refer to the Shema as the Jewish pledge of allegiance.]**

INTRODUCE THE NEW LETTER – ע

Point out the *ayin* on word card #21 and explain that this is another letter that is not sounded. Ask a student to come up to the *alef-bet* chart and point to another letter that is not sounded. **[*alef*]**

READING PRACTICE

Call on students to read the sounds on the three lines.

FYI

In the Sephardic tradition the *ayin* is pronounced as a guttural.

NOW READ & READ AGAIN

Call on students at random to read each of the lines. Encourage students to concentrate on their classmates' reading by having them follow the reading with their fingers. Suddenly stop the reading to see who has their finger at the correct spot. Praise those who have the place. Don't forget to recycle.

HERITAGE WORDS

The Hebrew word for "Hebrew" is עִבְרִית. Why is it important to learn how to read Hebrew? **[to be able to read the prayer book, Torah, etc.]**

What two words in line 8 seem to be related to the word שְׁמַע ? **[you will hear – תִּשְׁמַע, hearing – שְׁמִיעָה]**

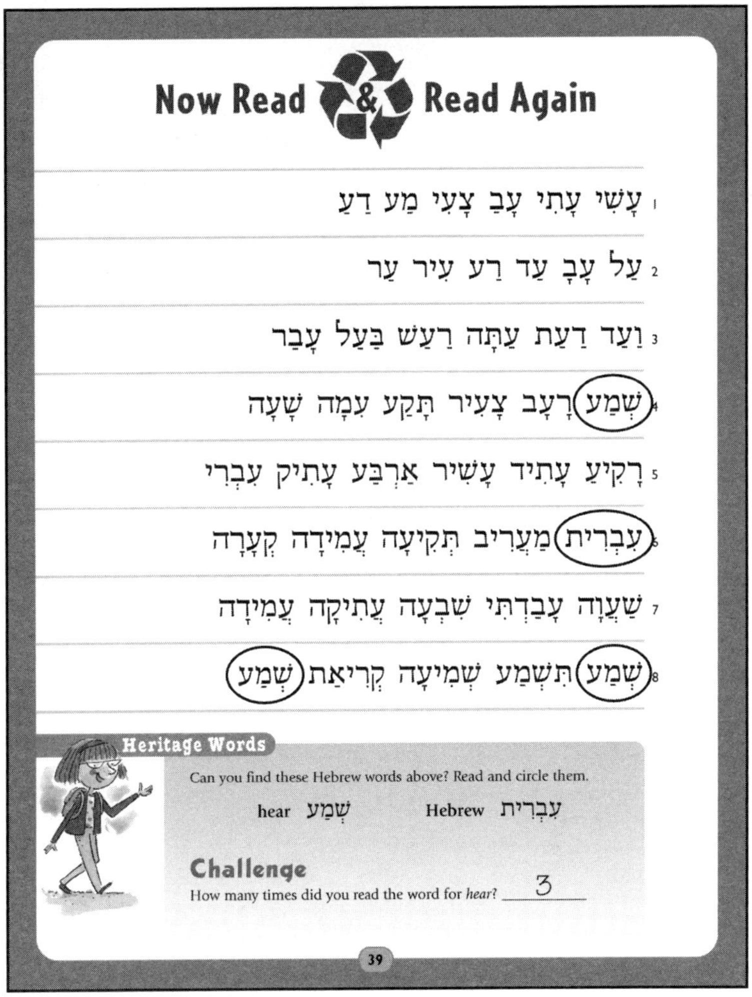

Now Read & Read Again

1 עָשִׂי עָתִי עָבַ צָעִי מַע דַעַ

2 עַל עָבָ עַד רַע עִיר עַר

3 וַעַד דַעַת עַתָּה רַעַשׁ בַּעַל עָבַר

4 שְׁמַע רָעָב צָעִיר תָּקַע עִמָּה שָׁעָה

5 רָקִיעַ עָתִיד עָשִׁיר אַרְבַּע עָתִיק עִבְרִי

6 עִבְרִית מַעֲרִיב תְּקִיעָה עֲמִידָה קְעָרָה

7 שַׁעֲוָה עָבַדְתִּי שִׁבְעָה עֲתִיקָה עֲמִידָה

8 שְׁמַע תִּשְׁמַע שְׁמִיעָה קְרִיאַת שְׁמַע

Heritage Words

Can you find these Hebrew words above? Read and circle them.

hear שְׁמַע   Hebrew עִבְרִית

Challenge

How many times did you read the word for *hear*? 3

39

Picture It in Hebrew

NEW LETTER ע

עוֹלָם

This photograph of the עוֹלָם was taken from outer space. Looking at the עוֹלָם from this distance, it is easy to imagine everyone working together for תִּיקוּן עוֹלָם —caring for the environment and all living things.

Put a check next to all of the ways you help take care of the עוֹלָם.

_____ recycle _____ care for a pet
_____ water plants _____ don't litter

Write another way you can help take care of the עוֹלָם.

World

Drumbeat

Draw a pair of drumsticks on each drum whose letter makes a sound.

How many pairs of drumsticks did you draw? 6

What sound does the letter make? ts

Tic-Tac-Toe

Play tic-tac-toe with a friend. Read the sounds correctly to make an X or an O.

3

רָ	מְ	הִי
בָ	דִ	כַ
עַ	צִ	אָ

2

עָ	כַ	תְ
וָ	הֱ	צִי
רִ	בְּ	קִ

1

בָ	תִי	קַ
לְ	אֱ	כִ
שַׁ	עַ	וִי

40

PICTURE IT IN HEBREW

Read the word עוֹלָם to the class. Call on several students to say the word while pointing to the photograph of the world.

Explain that *Tikkun Olam* means caring for the environment and all living things—literally "repairing the world." Ask students to find and underline the phrase תִּיקוּן עוֹלָם in the paragraph. Ask them to explain how they found the phrase. Students may respond that they found the English translation and worked backward to find the Hebrew, or that they were able to read part of the Hebrew.

This is a good time to remind the class that they are able to recognize many sounds, and are progressing quickly toward being able to read Hebrew fluently.

DRUMBEAT

After students have completed the exercise, play "Drumbeat Rhythm Reading." Choose a reading exercise in the book that the class has already learned. Decide whether the students will read in groups or individually. Tap a rhythm on your desk to set the pace as they read aloud. Then select students to drum the beat.

TIC-TAC-TOE

After students have completed this exercise, play tic-tac-toe as a class. Draw a tic-tac-toe grid on the chalkboard. Divide the class into two teams. To place an X or an O on the board, the students must correctly read an assigned line on a page that they have already learned.

ONLINE WORKBOOK

Assign activities from the online workbook and track your students' progress.

LESSON 10

Pages: 41–43
Key Word: נָבִיא
New Letters: נ ן
Alef-Bet Flashcards: 24, 25
Word Card: 23

KEY WORD (נָבִיא)

What is a prophet? **[In English the word "prophet" may mean someone with magical powers who can foretell the future. In Hebrew, the word *navi* means someone who speaks out as a messenger of God.]**

Why were the prophets important? **[They told us how God wanted us to behave, even if that message did not always please the Jewish people, and they gave hope to the Jewish people when they felt sad or confused.]**

Can you name any prophets? **[e.g., Moses, Elijah, Jeremiah, Isaiah, etc.]**

INTRODUCING THE NEW LETTERS – נ ן

Show word card #23 (נָבִיא) or print the word on the chalkboard and read it. Which letter in the word have they not learned? Display *alef-bet* flashcard #24 (נ) to the class and ask if any of the students know this letter. (A few may know the letter from the Ḥanukkah dreidel.) Teach the name of the letter and its sound.

Next, display *alef-bet* flashcard #25 (ן). Teach the name of this letter and its sound. Explain to students that *final nun* will be found only at the end of a word.

Occasionally some letters can be confusing to the students because of their similar appearance. Add flashcards #11, 12, 15, and 18 (ר כ ד ו) to the two new cards for this lesson and drill the students on these six look-alike letters.

READING PRACTICE

Read line 1 for the class and have them repeat the line in unison. Call on a student to read line 2 and then have the entire class repeat in unison. Repeat this procedure with line 3.

Now Read & Read Again

1 נָן נָו נְעִי קַן בִּין

2 נִין לָן דָן מָן שִׁין רָן

3 דִין בְּנִי עָנִי נָקִי אֲנִי נָא

4 שָׁנָה לָבָן עָנָו רִנָה עָנַד נַעַר

5 נָבִיא בִּינָה נְשָׁמָה מִשְׁנָה נְעָרָה

6 מַאֲמִין שְׁכִינָה כַּוָנָה נְעִילָה מַרְבִּין

7 רַעֲנָן מִשְׁכָּן לְהָבִין קַנְקַן לַמְדָן

8 נָבִיא מְדִינָה מַה נִשְׁתַּנָה נָבִיא

Heritage Word

Can you find this Hebrew word above? Read and circle it .

prophet נָבִיא

Challenge

At the Passover seder, the youngest child asks the Four Questions. Can you find the two Hebrew words in the lines above that introduce the Four Questions? Read and circle them.

42

NOW READ & READ AGAIN

Have a student read until you clap your hands. At that time, have the next student read. Determine the number of words according to the student's ability and reading fluency, keeping the pace lively.

HERITAGE WORDS

Which *navi* played a major role in the story of *Pesaḥ*? **[Moses]**

Which *navi* do we welcome into our homes during the Passover seder? Hint: We have a special cup for him to drink from. **[Elijah]**

PICTURE IT IN HEBREW

Students have learned all the letters and vowels in the word נְשִׁיקָה and should be encouraged to read it.

Demonstrate the word by blowing a kiss into the air and saying נְשִׁיקָה. Have students follow suit. Complete the activity together.

KNOCK, KNOCK

For a purposeful art project, have students make "doors" of their own in school or at home. You'll need the following: two sheets of unlined paper per student, crayons or markers, scissors, and glue sticks. On one sheet of paper, have students draw a door. To make it easy to open, be sure that the bottom of the door is at the bottom of the paper. Instruct them to cut along one side edge and the top edge of the door, and bend it back so that it opens. On the front of the door, students write one of the Hebrew words they have learned. On the back of the door, they write its English meaning. On the other sheet of paper, students draw a picture of the word they have chosen so that when the two sheets of paper are glued together, the door can open and the picture can be seen.

Mount the "doors" on your bulletin board for a fun, interactive display and for students to test one another's reading skills and Hebrew knowledge.

ONLINE WORKBOOK

Assign activities from the online workbook and track your students' progress.

NEW LETTER נ

Picture It in Hebrew

נְשִׁיקָה

Kiss

Giving someone a נְשִׁיקָה can mean "Hello, I'm happy to see you," or "Good-bye, I'll miss you!" What do you think this father's נְשִׁיקָה on his daughter's cheek is saying?

On Shabbat, when the Torah is carried around the sanctuary, people in the congregation give the Torah a נְשִׁיקָה. This is one way to show that they cherish the Torah. Describe how people in *your* congregation give the Torah a נְשִׁיקָה.

____

It is a custom to touch the special scroll which hangs on the doorpost of a Jewish home and give it a נְשִׁיקָה. Do you know what this scroll is called? Write its name here. mezuzah

Knock, Knock

Open the doors by writing the meaning of the Hebrew words on the door.

helper   hear   Shabbat   justice   blessing   commandment   bride

3 צְדָקָה justice
2 שַׁבָּת Shabbat
1 מִצְוָה commandment
7 בְּרָכָה blessing
6 שְׁמַע hear
5 שַׁמָּשׁ helper
4 כַּלָּה bride

43

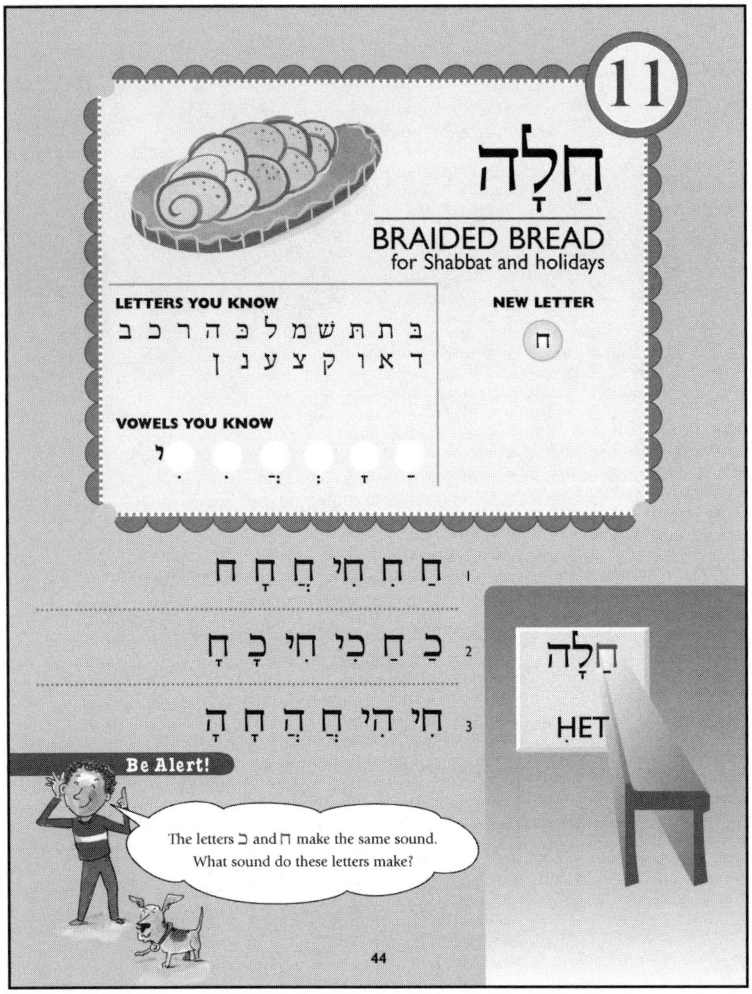

LESSON 11

Pages: 44–46
Key Word: חַלָּה
New Letter: ח
Alef-Bet Flashcard: 26
Word Cards: 24, 25

KEY WORD (חַלָּה)

Display word cards #1 (שַׁבָּת), #6 (בְּרָכָה), and #15 (מִצְוָה), and have the students read and define each word. Then ask, "What *brachah* do we recite on *Shabbat* to fulfill the *mitzvah* of eating *ḥallah*?"

בָּרוּךְ אַתָּה ה׳ אֱלֹהֵינוּ מֶלֶךְ הָעוֹלָם,
הַמּוֹצִיא לֶחֶם מִן הָאָרֶץ.

INTRODUCING THE NEW LETTER – ח

Print a large *hay* on the chalkboard and have the class identify the letter. Then print a large *ḥet* next to the *hay*. How do these two letters differ in appearance? Introduce the letter *ḥet*. What other letter is pronounced the same way? **[כ]**

Have the students look in their textbooks at the Key word. What is the first letter? **[*ḥet*]** Ask for a volunteer to read the word.

Take a poll. Who likes their *ḥallah* plain; with raisins; with poppy seeds; with sesame seeds? Does anyone else have a different favorite type of *ḥallah*?

FYI

Sephardic tradition distinguishes between the *ḥet* and the *chaf* by pronouncing the *ḥet* in a more guttural way.

READING PRACTICE

Randomly call on students to read each of these three lines. Remember, these lines can be repeated to give more students a chance to read.

NOW READ & READ AGAIN

Tape-record each student as he or she reads one of the lines. Two or three weeks later have the students, in the same order, read the same line on a second tape. Play back both and compare. This method allows the students to hear proof of their improvement.

HERITAGE WORDS

In what prayer do we use the word הָרַחֲמָן numerous times? **[*Birkat Hamazon* – Grace after Meals]**

Get a copy of *Birkat Hamazon* with translation and read to the students in Hebrew and then in English a few of the blessings that begin with the word *harahaman*. What other word usually begins a blessing? **[*baruch*]**

Now Read & Read Again

1 חִכָּ חָבִי חָתָ בָּח אַח צָח

2 חָל חִיל חַד חָשׁ חִישׁ חִימִי

3 קַח צַח נָח לָח אָח חַוָּה

4 חִכָּה שָׁכַח חָבִיב חֲבָל חָתָן לָקַח

5 חַלָּה חָלִיל וְצָחַק אַחַת חָצִיר חָנָן

6 מִנְחָה חֲמִשָּׁה שָׁלְחָה חִירִיק בָּחַרְתָּ

7 רַחֲמָן הָרַחֲמָן שַׁחֲרִית חֲתִימָה חֲדָשָׁה

8 הַחַלָּה הַבְּרָכָה חַלָּה לְשַׁבָּת הָרַחֲמָן

Heritage Words

Can you find these Hebrew words above? Read and circle them.

the Merciful One (God) הָרַחֲמָן — braided bread חַלָּה

Challenge

How many times did you read the word for *braided bread*? 2

45

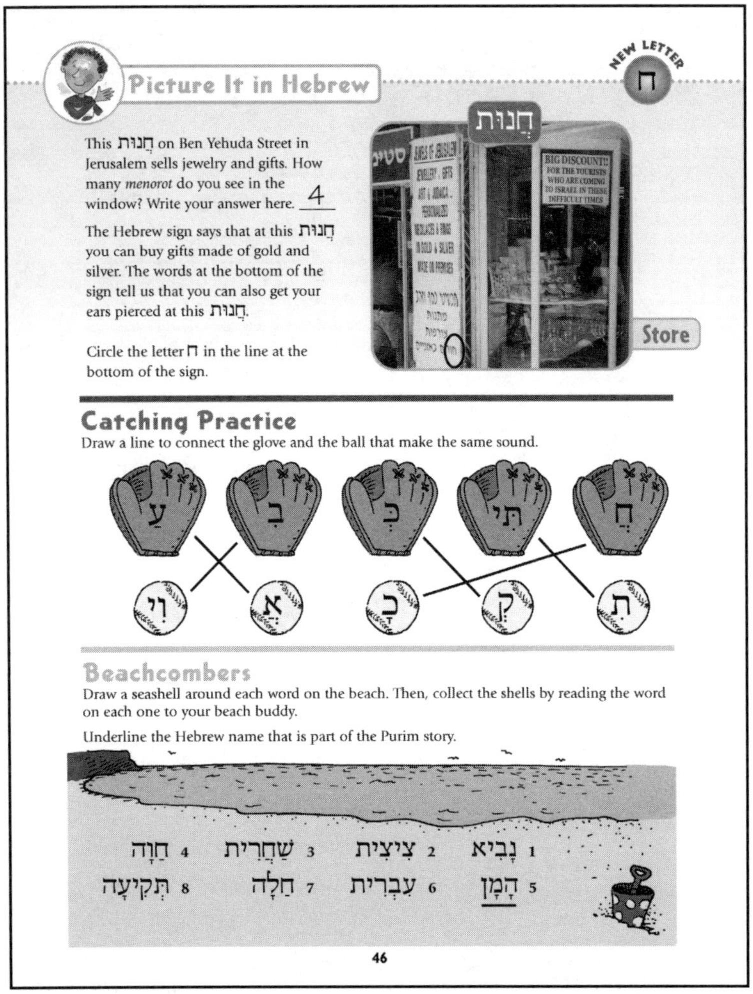

Picture It in Hebrew

NEW LETTER ח

This חֲנוּת on Ben Yehuda Street in Jerusalem sells jewelry and gifts. How many *menorot* do you see in the window? Write your answer here. 4

The Hebrew sign says that at this חֲנוּת you can buy gifts made of gold and silver. The words at the bottom of the sign tell us that you can also get your ears pierced at this חֲנוּת.

Circle the letter ח in the line at the bottom of the sign.

חֲנוּת

Store

Catching Practice

Draw a line to connect the glove and the ball that make the same sound.

עַ בּ כִּ תִּי חֵ

וִי אַ כָ קֵ תָ

Beachcombers

Draw a seashell around each word on the beach. Then, collect the shells by reading the word on each one to your beach buddy.

Underline the Hebrew name that is part of the Purim story.

1 נָבִיא 2 צִיצִית 3 שַׁחֲרִית 4 חַוָּה

5 הָמָן 6 עִבְרִית 7 חַלָּה 8 תְּקִיעָה

46

PICTURE IT IN HEBREW

Read the word חֲנוּת to the class. Ask students to name their favorite חֲנוּת. Have students identify the first letter and sound of חֲנוּת. **[ḥet, ḥ]** Have students complete the activity individually, then review it together.

CATCHING PRACTICE

To extend this exercise, you will need a soft ball. Select a page in the book that the students have already learned. Gently toss or roll the ball to a student; have that student read a designated line and then return the ball. Repeat until all of the students have had a turn to read.

BEACHCOMBERS

After students have read aloud in pairs, have one beach buddy say the English meaning of any word in the exercise, and the other say the word in Hebrew. Then switch roles.

ONLINE WORKBOOK

Assign activities from the online workbook and track your students' progress.

LESSON 12

Pages: 47–49
Key Word: עֲלִיָּה
New Letter: י
Alef-Bet Flashcard: 27
Word Cards: 26, 27

KEY WORD (עֲלִיָּה)

- What does it mean when someone receives an עֲלִיָּה to the Torah? **[They will recite the blessings before and after the ritual reading of the Torah in the synagogue.]**
- Why do you think being called up to recite the blessings over the Torah is called *aliyah* – going up? Where is the Torah read from? **[the *bimah*]** How do you get to the *bimah*? **[walk up several steps]** We are raised up spiritually when we are honored by reciting the blessings over the Torah.

INTRODUCING THE NEW LETTER – י

Print the Key word on the chalkboard. Are there any letters or vowels in the word that the students have not seen before? **[no]** Point to the *yud* and ask what vowel this is part of. **[*ḥirik* – ◌ִי]** Explain that in addition to being part of a vowel sound, the *yud* can also stand alone as a letter. Demonstrate the sound of the *yud* and then read the Key word to the class.

Hold up *alef-bet* flashcards #11, 18, and 25 (ר ו ן) next to *alef-bet* flashcard #27 (י). Ask how each of these letters differs from the *yud.* How can you tell when the *yud* is part of a vowel and when it stands alone as a letter? **[The *yud* is read as a letter when it has a vowel directly underneath it. E.g., יָ vs. אִי]** Remember to also teach the pronunciation of the sound pattern יִי.

READING PRACTICE

Randomly call on students to read each of these three lines. Remember, these lines can be repeated to give more students a chance to read.

12

עֲלִיָּה
GOING UP
the honor of being called up to recite the blessings over the Torah

LETTERS YOU KNOW
בּ ת תּ שׁ מ ל כּ ה ר כ ב
ד א ו ק צ ע נ ן ח

NEW LETTER
י

VOWELS YOU KNOW
ַ ָ ְ ֲ ִ ִי

עֲלִיָּה
YUD

1 יַ יָ יִ יִי יְ יָ

2 יַ וַ יְ וְ יִי וִי

3 יָשָׁ יָר יִן יְשִׁי חַיִ יְדִי

47

Now Read & Read Again

1 יָד יְהִי יַיִן יַמִּי יָדַי יָמָה

2 שִׁישׁ יָשָׁן מִיָּד נְיָר לַיִל הֲיִי

3 בַּיִת יָשָׁר יַעַר חַיָּה עַיִן יָשַׁב

4 יָדַע אַיִל חַיָּב יָחִיד יָקָר מַעְיָן

5 יְצִיר הָיָה יָוָן חַיִל יָצָא עֲדַיִן

6 יַחְדָו יִרְאָה יִצְחָק יַבָּשָׁה צִיַּרְתִּי

7 עֲלִיָּה כְּוִיָּה יוֹכַח יַלְדָּה יְדִיעָה

8 יְשִׁיבָה יִשְׁתַּבַּח הָיְתָה מִנְיָן עֲלִיָּה

Heritage Words

Can you find these Hebrew words above? Read and circle them.

aliyah, going up עֲלִיָּה

ten Jewish adults, the minimum needed for a prayer service מִנְיָן

Challenge

How many times did you read the word for *aliyah*? 2

48

NOW READ & READ AGAIN

Have students read three words at a time. The first student reads three words. The second student overlaps by beginning with the previous student's last word.

HERITAGE WORDS

A מִנְיָן is needed for the Torah to be read and therefore for someone to receive an *aliyah* to the Torah.

Why are there certain rituals or prayers that can be done only with a *minyan*? **[Ten people represent a community. There are some rituals and prayers that are so important, we want to do them only when a community of people is present. Also, by praying in a group we think about other people as well as ourselves.]**

PICTURE IT IN HEBREW

Read the phrase יוֹם הוּלֶדֶת to the class. Ask individual students when their יוֹם הוּלֶדֶת is.

Teach students to say "Happy Birthday" in Hebrew. (יוֹם הוּלֶדֶת שָׂמֵחַ—*yom huledet same'aḥ*). Sing "Happy Birthday" in Hebrew to a student who has recently celebrated a birthday or will soon do so.

HAND IN HAND

After students have completed the exercise, add a fun challenge. One student in each pair holds up a number of fingers, and the other student reads the word on the hand corresponding to that number. Students take turns until they have each read all the words at least once.

ONLINE WORKBOOK

Assign activities from the online workbook and track your students' progress.

NEW LETTER ו

Picture It in Hebrew

יוֹם הוּלֶדֶת

You don't have to be a child to celebrate your יוֹם הוּלֶדֶת with a cake and party hats! In Israel it's the custom to lift up the person celebrating his or her יוֹם הוּלֶדֶת in a chair while singing "הַיּוֹם יוֹם הוּלֶדֶת" which means "Today is the birthday."

When is your יוֹם הוּלֶדֶת? Write your answer here.

____

Birthday

Hand in Hand

Read the word on each hand to a classmate. Then listen to your classmate read. Shake hands when you're done!

1 יִצְחָק
2 מִנְיָן
3 עֲלִיָּה
4 יָד
5 נָבִיא
6 הַשְּׁבִיעִי
7 הַלַּיְלָה
8 קָדִימָה
9 שִׁירָה
10 עַיִן
11 בְּרִית
12 צַדִּיק

49

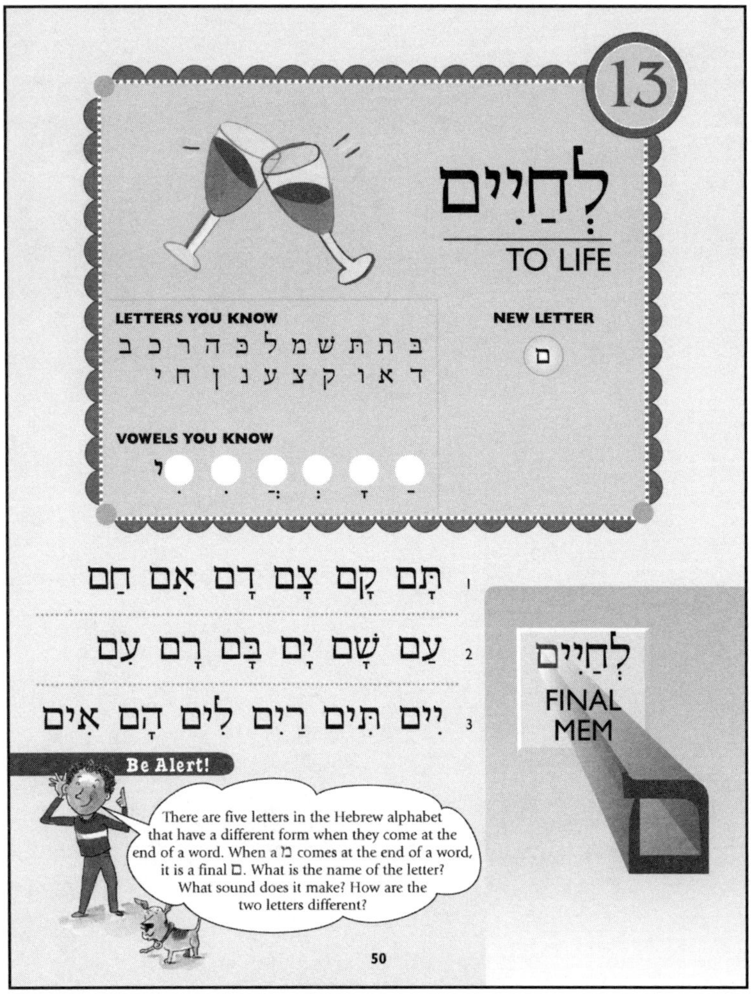

13

לְחַיִּים

TO LIFE

LETTERS YOU KNOW

בּ ת תּ שׁ מ ל כּ ה ר כ ב

ד א ו ק צ ע נ ן ח י

NEW LETTER

ם

VOWELS YOU KNOW

1 תָּם קָם צָם דָם אִם חַם

2 עַם שָׁם יָם בָּם רָם עִם

3 יִים תִּים רַיִם לִים הָם אִים

לְחַיִּים

FINAL MEM

Be Alert!

There are five letters in the Hebrew alphabet that have a different form when they come at the end of a word. When a מ comes at the end of a word, it is a final ם. What is the name of the letter? What sound does it make? How are the two letters different?

50

LESSON 13

Pages: 50–53
Key Word: לְחַיִּים
New Letter: ם
Alef-Bet Flashcard: 28
Word Cards: 28, 29, 30

REVIEW EXERCISE

Utilizing the Key and Heritage words learned up to this point, post a column of at least six words. Individuals or teams take turns "climbing the ladder" by reading and translating the words on the ladder. Score one point for each word read correctly and an additional two points for each word translated correctly.

INTRODUCING THE NEW LETTER – ם

Ask the students which letter has a special form that is used only as the last letter in a word. **[ן]** Then point to the *mem* on the *alef-bet* chart and ask for a volunteer to identify it. Explain that the *mem* also has a special form used only at the end of a word and then point to the *final mem* on the *alef-bet* chart.

KEY WORD (לְחַיִּים)

Print the word לְחַיִּים on the chalkboard or show word card #28 and ask for a volunteer to read it. Is this word familiar to anyone? Explain that *l'ḥayyim* is not actually a word, but a phrase. Put one circle around the לְ and another one around חַיִּים. Explain that לְ is the preposition meaning "to" and חַיִּים means "life."

You may want to ask the challenge question found at the bottom of the following page at this time. "When would you say *l'ḥayyim?*"

READING PRACTICE

Call on students randomly to read each of the three lines.

NOW READ & READ AGAIN

Change the line sequence by first reading all the odd-numbered lines followed by the even-numbered lines.

HERITAGE WORDS

In some contexts the word אָדָם refers to humans in general, and not only males. This is similar to statements such as "All men are created equal," which refers to all humanity.

What was the name of the first woman? **[Eve – חַוָּה – who gave birth (life) to future generations.]**

Why do we recall יְצִיאַת מִצְרַיִם every Shabbat? Indeed, it is part of many of our Shabbat prayers, including the Kiddush. **[The verse from the Ten Commandments telling us to observe Shabbat says that we should "remember that you were a slave in the land of Egypt and that *Adonai*, your God, set you free." As slaves the Israelites had no day of rest.]**

Now Read & Read Again

1 הָלַם אַחִים עָלִים מְרָיִם בַּדִּים תָּרַם

2 אִיִּים שְׁנַיִם בָּתִּים אָדָם דַּקִּים מִצְרַיִם

3 חָכָם רַעַם יָמִים רַבִּים חַיִּים דָּמַם

4 בָּנִים מַיִם אָדָם שְׁתַּיִם מִלִּים אָשָׁם

5 נָשִׁים שָׁמַיִם דְּבָרִים יָדַיִם קָמִים עָלִים

6 אַבְרָהָם נְבִיאִים כְּרָמִים שִׁבְעִים אֲנָשִׁים

7 עִבְרִים רַחֲמִים יְלָדִים צַדִּיקִים מְלָכִים

8 עֲבָדִים יְצִיאַת מִצְרַיִם לְחַיִּים לְחַיִּים

Heritage Words

Can you find these Hebrew words above? Read and circle them.

to life לְחַיִּים

the name of the first human (man) אָדָם

the Exodus, going out from Egypt יְצִיאַת מִצְרַיִם

Challenge

Jewish people say לְחַיִּים on very special occasions.

When would you say לְחַיִּים?

51

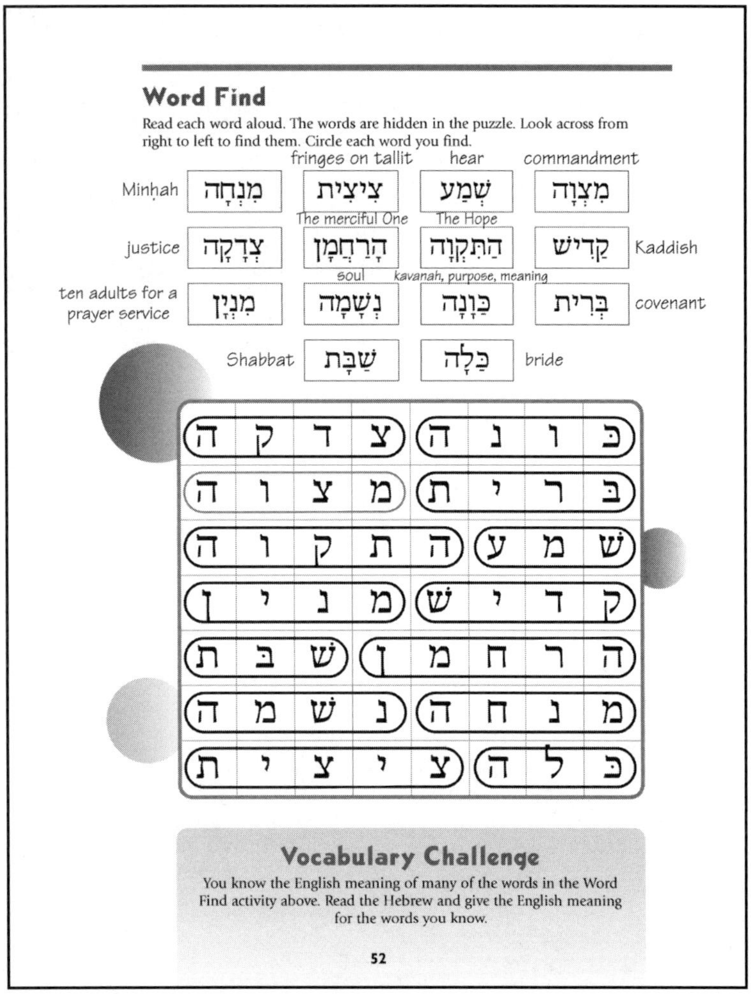

Word Find

Read each word aloud. The words are hidden in the puzzle. Look across from right to left to find them. Circle each word you find.

Minḥah מִנְחָה	fringes on tallit צִיצִית	hear שְׁמַע	commandment מִצְוָה
justice צְדָקָה	The merciful One הָרַחֲמָן	The Hope הַתִּקְוָה	Kaddish קַדִּישׁ
ten adults for a prayer service מִנְיָן	soul נְשָׁמָה	kavanah, purpose, meaning כַּוָּנָה	covenant בְּרִית
	Shabbat שַׁבָּת	bride כַּלָּה	

ה	ק	ד	צ	ה	נ	ו	כּ
ה	ו	צ	מ	ת	י	ר	בּ
ה	ו	ק	ת	ה	ע	מ	שׁ
ן	י	נ	מ	שׁ	י	ד	ק
ת	ב	שׁ	ן	מ	ח	ר	ה
ה	מ	שׁ	נ	ה	ח	נ	מ
ת	י	צ	י	צ	ה	ל	כּ

Vocabulary Challenge

You know the English meaning of many of the words in the Word Find activity above. Read the Hebrew and give the English meaning for the words you know.

52

WORD FIND

Call on students to read each of the words. Before class, copy the puzzle onto the chalkboard and call on students individually to come to the board and circle one of the words on the list.

Then have students complete the activity in their books.

PICTURE IT IN HEBREW

Students have learned all the letters and vowels in the word מַיִם and should be encouraged to read it. Call on individual students to read the paragraphs.

Ask if they remember the word לְחַיִּים. **["to life!"]** When do we say לְחַיִּים? **[when we're making a toast]**

WORD POWER

In addition to circling the appropriate word on each line, have the students put a square around all the other words that have been taught as key words in this book.

ḥallah; braided braid – חַלָּה
havdalah; separation – הַבְדָּלָה
helper – שַׁמָּשׁ
commandment – מִצְוָה
prophet – נָבִיא

ONLINE WORKBOOK

Assign activities from the online workbook and track your students' progress.

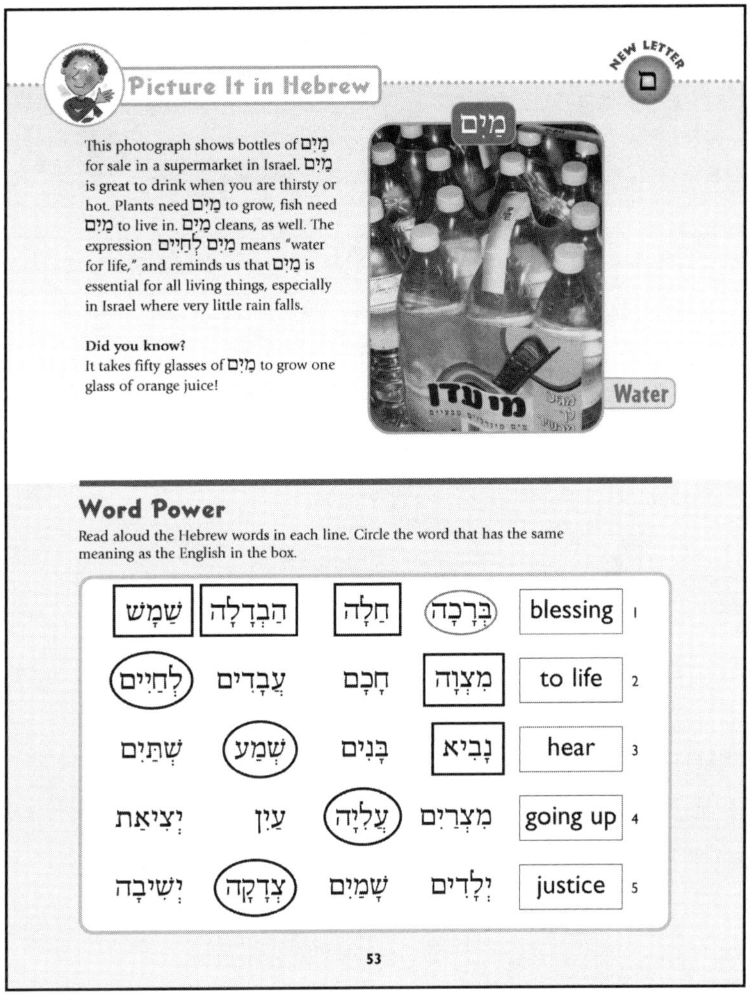
Picture It in Hebrew

New Letter ם

מַיִם

This photograph shows bottles of מַיִם for sale in a supermarket in Israel. מַיִם is great to drink when you are thirsty or hot. Plants need מַיִם to grow, fish need מַיִם to live in. מַיִם cleans, as well. The expression מַיִם לְחַיִּים means "water for life," and reminds us that מַיִם is essential for all living things, especially in Israel where very little rain falls.

Did you know?
It takes fifty glasses of מַיִם to grow one glass of orange juice!

Water

Word Power

Read aloud the Hebrew words in each line. Circle the word that has the same meaning as the English in the box.

שַׁמָּשׁ	הַבְדָּלָה	חַלָּה	בְּרָכָה	blessing	1
לְחַיִּים	עֲבָדִים	חָכָם	מִצְוָה	to life	2
שְׁתַּיִם	שְׁמַע	בָּנִים	נָבִיא	hear	3
יְצִיאַת	עַיִן	עֲלִיָּה	מִצְרַיִם	going up	4
יְשִׁיבָה	צְדָקָה	שָׁמַיִם	יְלָדִים	justice	5

53

14

תּוֹרָה

TORAH

LETTERS YOU KNOW

ב ת תּ ש מ ל כּ ה ר כ ב

ד א ו ק צ ע נ ן ח י ם

VOWELS YOU KNOW

NEW VOWELS

1 תּוֹ בּוֹ רוֹ מוֹ לוֹ דוֹ נוֹ

2 א צ ק ע נ ח י

3 מֹעַ עוֹת אָנ שׁוֹן קֹב דוֹשׁ

Be Alert!

Usually a vowel is found below a letter: רָ, שְׁ.
But the vowel וֹ or ֹ follows a letter: תּוֹ מֹ

תּוֹרָה

54

LESSON 14

Pages: 54–56
Key Word: תּוֹרָה
New Vowels: וֹ ◌ֹ
Alef-Bet Flashcards: 29, 30
Word Cards: 31, 32, 33, 34, 35, 36

REVIEW EXERCISE

Using the chalkboard or flannelboard, review the seven letters used in line 1 on page 54 (without the vowel). Review the vowels learned so far by placing each one in turn with each letter. Have students take turns reading the sounds.

KEY WORD (תּוֹרָה)

Ask what the picture is at the beginning of the lesson. How do you feel when you see the Torah? Why do we regularly read the Torah out loud in the synagogue? **[so that everyone has the opportunity to hear it and so that its stories and laws will not be forgotten]**

Sing the song *Torah Tzivah Lanu Moshe.*

INTRODUCING THE NEW VOWELS – (*ḤOLAM*: ◌ֹ וֹ)

Using *alef-bet* flashcards #29 and #30, show the new vowel *ḥolam* to students. Then add the *alef-bet* flashcards for the other vowels learned, review, and drill them. (5, 6, 13, 16, 21, 22) Display and read word card #31 (תּוֹרָה). Have the students identify each letter and vowel.

READING PRACTICE

Call on students at random to read lines 1–3.

NOW READ & READ AGAIN

Call on students randomly to read each line. Don't forget to recycle the exercise!

HERITAGE WORDS

How do we greet each other on Shabbat? **[שַׁבַּת שָׁלוֹם]**

What is the difference between the *ḥallah* we use on Shabbat and the one we make for רֹאשׁ הַשָּׁנָה? **[On Shabbat it is braided and on Rosh Hashanah it is round.]** Is the blessing the same? **[Yes]** Can you recite the blessing over bread? What does it mean? **[Praised are You, *Adonai* our God, Ruler of the universe, who brings forth bread from the earth.]** הַמּוֹצִיא literally means "the one who brings forth."

What do we do to show that the Torah is a holy object? **[dress it with ornaments, kiss it, keep it in the Ark, stand when the ark is open, etc.]**

Now Read & Read Again

1 כֹּל לֹא אוֹת יוֹם חוֹל צֹאן

2 עוֹד קוֹל מוֹת שׁוֹר צוֹם חוֹר

3 שָׁמֹעַ יָבֹא אֹתָם דָתוֹ אָנֹכִי כְּמוֹ

4 אָבוֹת מְאֹד כְּבוֹד לָשׁוֹן נָכוֹן שָׁעוֹת

5 קָדוֹשׁ תּוֹרָה צִיּוֹן מוֹרָה תְּהֹם מְלֹא

6 שְׁלֹמֹה אַהֲרֹן יַעֲקֹב אֲדוֹן עוֹלָם

7 הַמּוֹצִיא שַׁבַּת שָׁלוֹם רֹאשׁ הַשָּׁנָה

8 תּוֹרָה בְּרָכוֹת מִצְוֹת דוֹרוֹת כֹּהֲנִים

Heritage Words

Can you find these Hebrew words above? Read and circle them.

Torah, teaching	תּוֹרָה	a peaceful Shabbat	שַׁבַּת שָׁלוֹם
holy	קָדוֹשׁ	blessing over bread	הַמּוֹצִיא
hello, good-bye, peace	שָׁלוֹם	Jewish New Year	רֹאשׁ הַשָּׁנָה

Challenge

Can you find the name of the Jewish New Year in the words above? Circle it.
Can you recite the בְּרָכָה we say over bread?

55

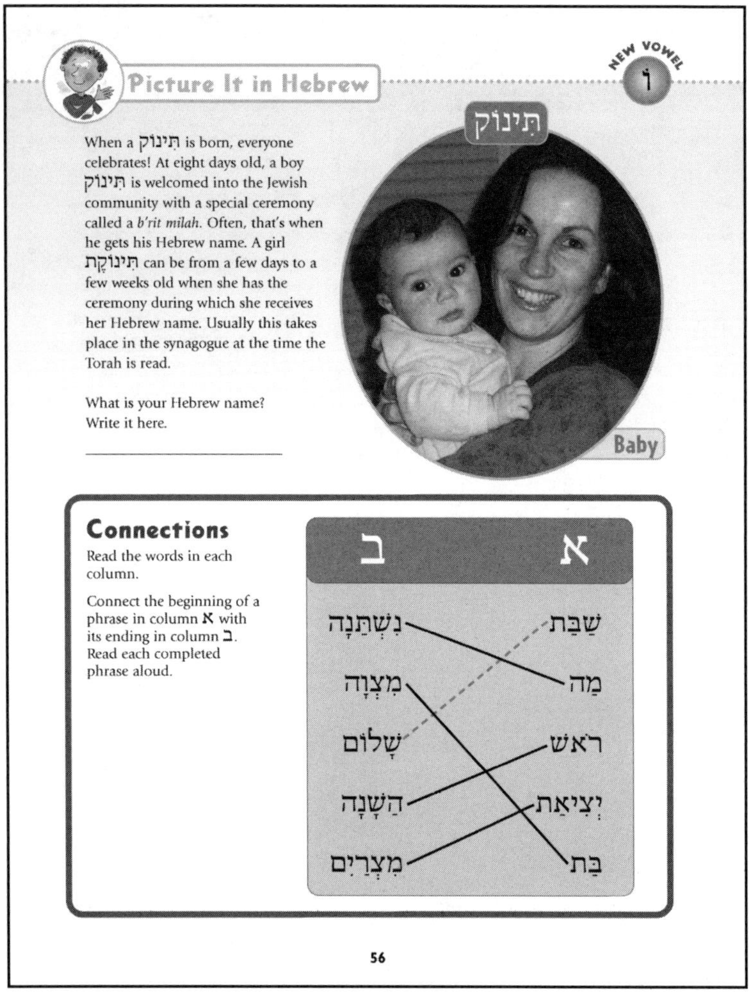

When a תִּינוֹק is born, everyone celebrates! At eight days old, a boy תִּינוֹק is welcomed into the Jewish community with a special ceremony called a *b'rit milah*. Often, that's when he gets his Hebrew name. A girl תִּינוֹקֶת can be from a few days to a few weeks old when she has the ceremony during which she receives her Hebrew name. Usually this takes place in the synagogue at the time the Torah is read.

What is your Hebrew name?
Write it here.

____

Connections

Read the words in each column.

Connect the beginning of a phrase in column א with its ending in column ב. Read each completed phrase aloud.

ב	א
נִשְׁתַּנָּה	שַׁבַּת
מִצְוָה	מַה
שָׁלוֹם	רֹאשׁ
הַשָּׁנָה	יְצִיאַת
מִצְרַיִם	בַּת

56

PICTURE IT IN HEBREW

Students have learned all the letters and vowels in the word תִּינוֹק and should be encouraged to read it. Help them to read the word תִּינוֹקֶת when you encounter it in the paragraph.

Help students to write their Hebrew names on the blank line in the activity. Ask for volunteers to come up to the board to write their names in Hebrew.

CONNECTIONS

Have the students complete this exercise independently. Then call on one student to read the beginning word of a phrase and another student to read the concluding word of that phrase.

Another option is to play a matching game. Distribute cards with the beginning of the phrase to some students and cards with the ending of the phrase to the other students. Students find a match for their part of the phrase. At the end of the game, everyone should be standing in pairs.

ONLINE WORKBOOK

Assign activities from the online workbook and track your students' progress.

LESSON 15

Pages: 57–59
Key Word: טַלִּית
New Letter: ט
Alef-Bet Flashcard: 31
Word Cards: 37, 38, 39

REVIEW EXERCISE

Tic-Tac-Toe

Play "tic-tac-toe" as described in #4 on page vii. Use *alef-bet* flashcards #1–30.

KEY WORD (טַלִּית)

Have the students look at the picture of the Key word and then identify it. What sound does the first letter have? **[t]**

When is the *tallit* worn? **[During morning services. It is worn every day, including Shabbat and holidays.]** When is a *tallit* worn at night? **[Kol Nidrei service on Yom Kippur eve]**

INTRODUCING THE NEW LETTER – ט

Display word card #37 (טַלִּית) and teach the letter *tet*. Have students identify each of the letters in the word. Did anyone identify the *tet* as being a *mem*? This is a common error.

What letter has the same sound as the *tet*? **[*tav*]** What other letters in the Hebrew alphabet have sound-alike letters? **[א=ע, ב=ו, כ=ח]**

Since *mem* and *tet* are often confused, point to the *mem* on the *alef-bet* chart, have the students identify it, and ask the students to describe the difference in appearance between the *mem* and *tet*. A helpful hint for the students is that "*mem* has a man standing on a mountain (מ); *tet* is open on the top (ט)."

15
טַלִּית
TALLIT, PRAYER SHAWL

LETTERS YOU KNOW
בּ ת תּ שׁ מ ל כּ ה ר כ ב
ד א ו ק צ ע נ ן ח י ם

NEW LETTER
ט

VOWELS YOU KNOW

1 טַ טְ טִ טוֹ טִי טֹ
2 טוֹ מוֹ טָ מָ טְ מְ
3 טָה טַשׁ בָּט עַט טָר נְטִי

טַלִּית
TET

57

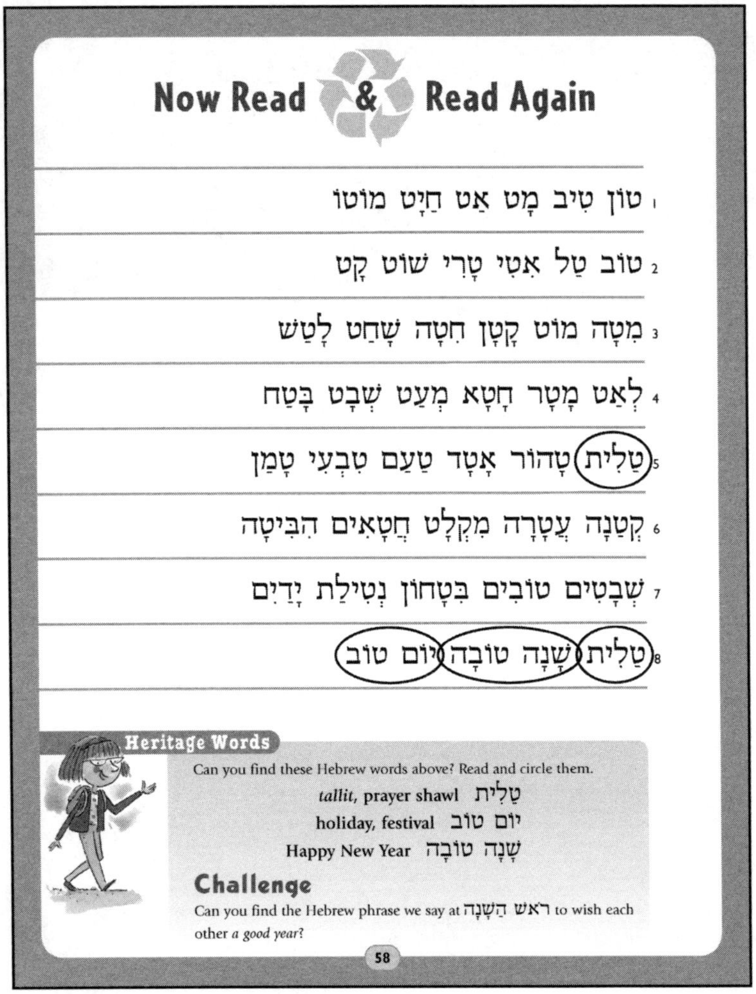

Now Read & Read Again

1 טוֹן טִיב מָט אַט חַיָט מוֹטוֹ

2 טוֹב טַל אִטִי טָרִי שׁוֹט קָט

3 מִטָה מוֹט קָטָן חִטָה שָׁחַט לָטַשׁ

4 לְאַט מָטָר חָטָא מְעַט שְׁבָט בָּטַח

5 טַלִית טָהוֹר אָטָד טַעַם טִבְעִי טָמַן

6 קְטַנָּה עֲטָרָה מִקְלָט חֲטָאִים הַבַּיְתָה

7 שְׁבָטִים טוֹבִים בִּטָחוֹן נְטִילַת יָדַיִם

8 טַלִית שָׁנָה טוֹבָה יוֹם טוֹב

Heritage Words

Can you find these Hebrew words above? Read and circle them.

tallit, prayer shawl טַלִית

holiday, festival יוֹם טוֹב

Happy New Year שָׁנָה טוֹבָה

Challenge

Can you find the Hebrew phrase we say at רֹאשׁ הַשָּׁנָה to wish each other *a good year*?

58

NOW READ & READ AGAIN

Return to the tic-tac-toe game and have students from each team alternate reading the lines of reading practice. Correct reading of a line allows that team to place a letter on the tic-tac-toe board. To give more students a chance to read, have each student read only two or three words at a time.

HERITAGE WORDS

יוֹם טוֹב literally means "good day." Why do you think this phrase is used for "holiday" or "festival"?

PICTURE IT IN HEBREW

The word טֶלֶפוֹן should be easy for students to understand since it sounds so similar to "telephone." (It is a cognate.) Say the word several times and have students repeat it after you. Ask students the name and sound of the first letter in the word. **[*tet,* t]**

Enrichment: Teach students the numbers 1–10 in Hebrew.

ahat	אַחַת	1.
shtayim	שְׁתַּיִים	2.
shalosh	שָׁלוֹשׁ	3.
arba	אַרְבַּע	4.
hameish	חָמֵשׁ	5.
sheish	שֵׁשׁ	6.
sheva	שֶׁבַע	7.
shmoneh	שְׁמוֹנֶה	8.
teisha	תֵּשַׁע	9.
eser	עֶשֶׂר	10.

EREV SHABBAT

Expand the activity by making several sets of flame-shaped cards from yellow construction paper. There should be ten cards per set, with a letter on each one: ח ב א כּ ו ט כ ע ת ק. Students can play Concentration or Go Fish, pairing the letters that sound alike.

MIX AND MATCH

Have the students complete this exercise independently.

ONLINE WORKBOOK

Assign activities from the online workbook and track your students' progress.

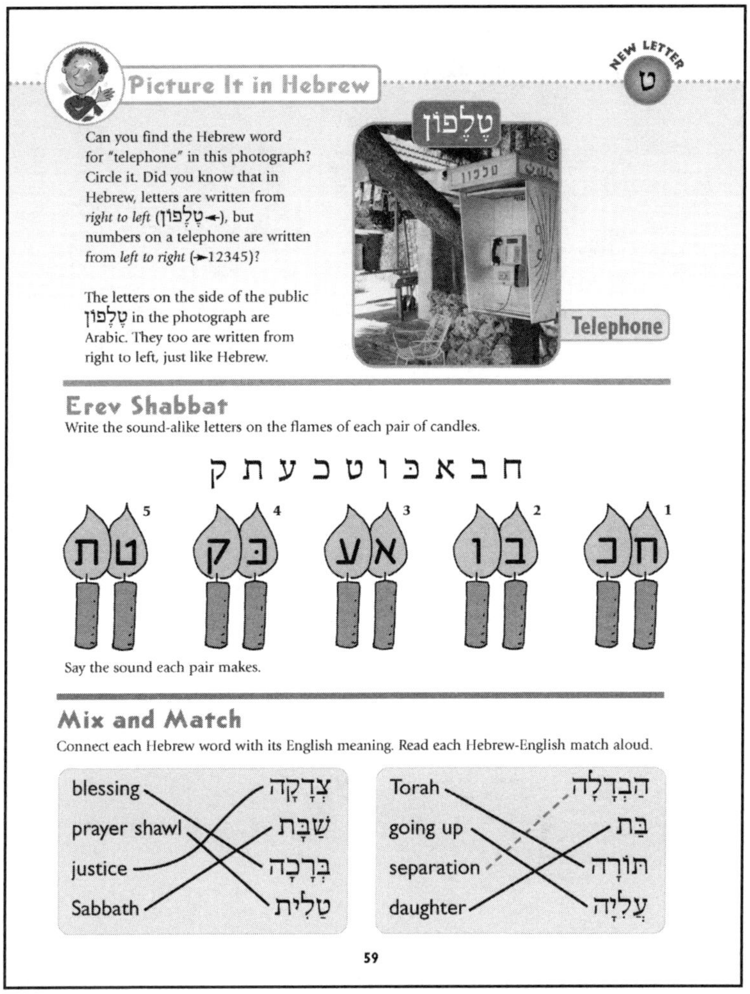
Picture It in Hebrew

NEW LETTER ט

טֶלֶפוֹן

Can you find the Hebrew word for "telephone" in this photograph? Circle it. Did you know that in Hebrew, letters are written from *right to left* (טֶלֶפוֹן←), but numbers on a telephone are written from *left to right* (→12345)?

The letters on the side of the public טֶלֶפוֹן in the photograph are Arabic. They too are written from right to left, just like Hebrew.

Telephone

Erev Shabbat

Write the sound-alike letters on the flames of each pair of candles.

ח ב א כּ ו ט כ ע ת ק

1 ח כ — 2 ב ו — 3 א ע — 4 כּ ק — 5 ט ת

Say the sound each pair makes.

Mix and Match

Connect each Hebrew word with its English meaning. Read each Hebrew-English match aloud.

blessing	צְדָקָה
prayer shawl	שַׁבָּת
justice	בְּרָכָה
Sabbath	טַלִּית

Torah	הַבְדָּלָה
going up	בַּת
separation	תּוֹרָה
daughter	עֲלִיָּה

59

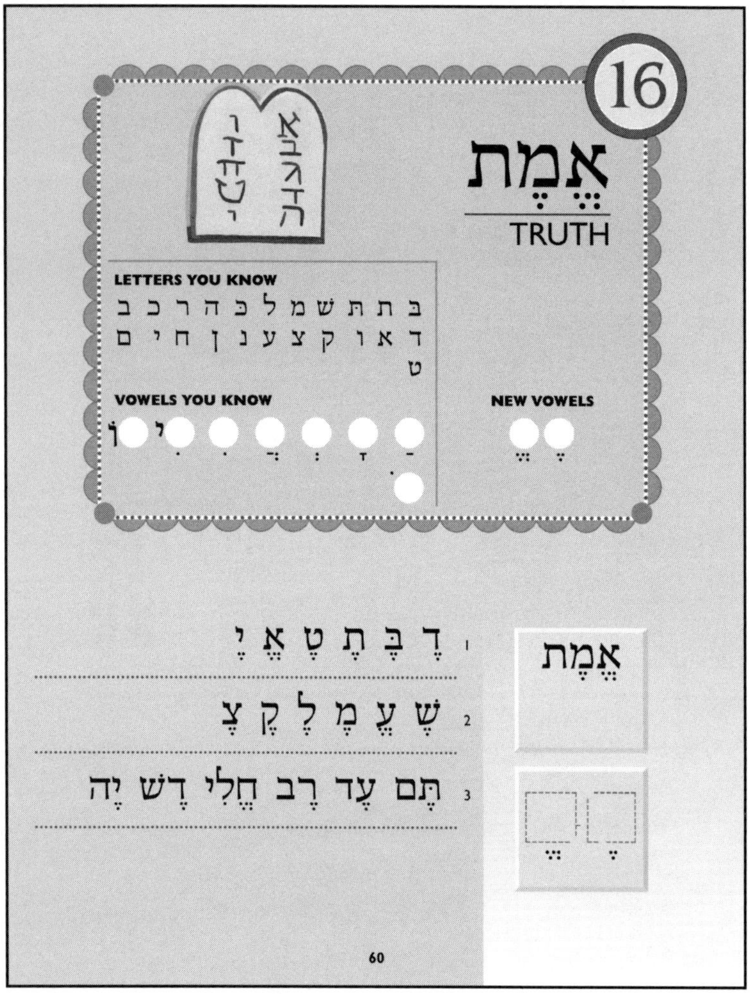

16

אֱמֶת

TRUTH

LETTERS YOU KNOW

בּ ת תּ שׁ מ ל כּ ה ר כ ב

ד א ו ק צ ע נ ן ח י ם

ט

VOWELS YOU KNOW

NEW VOWELS

1 דֶ בֶ תֶ טֶ אֱ יֶ

2 שֶׁ עֱ מֶ לֶ קֶ צֶ

3 תֶם עֶד רֶב חֱלִי דֶשׁ יֶה

אֱמֶת

60

LESSON 16

Pages: 60–62
Key Word: אֱמֶת
New Vowels: ◌ֶ ◌ֱ
Alef-Bet Flashcards: 32, 33
Word Cards: 40, 41, 42, 43

KEY WORD (אֱמֶת)

Print אֱמֶת on the chalkboard and ask for a volunteer to identify each of the letters. Read the word aloud and ask the students what sound they think this vowel makes. Define the word for the students. *Emet* means truth. People must speak *emet* when dealing with one another. *Emet* is also part of the nature of God. That is to say, God represents truth.

Are there times when it would be acceptable not to tell the truth?

What is a "white lie"? Is it acceptable to tell "white lies"? **[Our tradition does not consider it wrong to tell a "white lie." For example, it is permitted to tell a lie in order to avoid strife and contention. Of course, common sense must be a guiding principle.]**

INTRODUCING THE NEW VOWELS – (*SEGOL*: ◌ֶ and *ḤATAF SEGOL*: ◌ֱ)

Display *alef-bet* flashcard #32 (◌ֶ) and introduce this vowel and its sound. Hold *alef-bet* flashcards #13 (◌ֵ) and #21 (◌ִ) next to the *segol* and ask how the *segol* differs in sound and appearance.

Display *alef-bet* flashcard #33 (◌ֱ) and ask what two vowels are seen here. **[*segol* and *shvah*]** What other vowel also contains "two vowels in one?" **[*ḥataf pataḥ*]** Explain that just as in the case of the *ḥataf pataḥ*, the *shvah* does not change the pronunciation of the primary vowel.

READING PRACTICE

Read line 1 for the class and have them repeat the line in unison. Call on a student to read line 2 and then have the entire class repeat in unison. Repeat this procedure with line 3.

NOW READ & READ AGAIN

Have one student read a line and then call out another line number for the next student to read.

HERITAGE WORDS

What object do we keep in the אֲרוֹן הַקֹּדֶשׁ? **[Torah]**

In what blessing do we recite the phrase הַמּוֹצִיא לֶחֶם? **[the blessing over bread]**

Why do you think that a drawing of the tablets of the Ten Commandments was chosen to represent the word אֱמֶת at the top of the previous page? **[You shall not lie is one of the Ten Commandments; the Ten Commandments are from God, and God represents truth; etc.]**

Now Read & Read Again

1 אֶת אֶל שֶׁלִי שֶׁלֹא אֱמֶת אַתֶּן

2 אֲשֶׁר שֶׁמֶשׁ יֶלֶד לָכֶם אֹהֶל אֶבֶן

3 אַתֶּם נֶצַח חֹדֶשׁ כֹּתֶל טֶרֶם אֶחָד

4 רוֹצֶה שֶׁבַע עֶרֶב מוֹרֶה נֶאֱמָן יִהְיֶה

5 וְנֶאֱמַר מְחַיֶּה רוֹעֶה עוֹלֶה הֶחֱלִיט שְׁמוֹנֶה

6 לְעוֹלָם וָעֶד תּוֹרַת אֱמֶת מְצַוֶּה אֶתְכֶם

7 אֲרוֹן הַקֹּדֶשׁ כֶּתֶר תּוֹרָה וַיֹּאמֶר אֱלֹהִים

8 אֱלֹהִים הַמּוֹצִיא לֶחֶם אֱמֶת וָצֶדֶק

Heritage Words

Can you find these Hebrew words above? Read and circle them.

truth אֱמֶת — Who brings forth bread הַמּוֹצִיא לֶחֶם

God אֱלֹהִים — the Holy Ark אֲרוֹן הַקֹּדֶשׁ

Challenge

How many times did you read the word for *truth*? 3

61

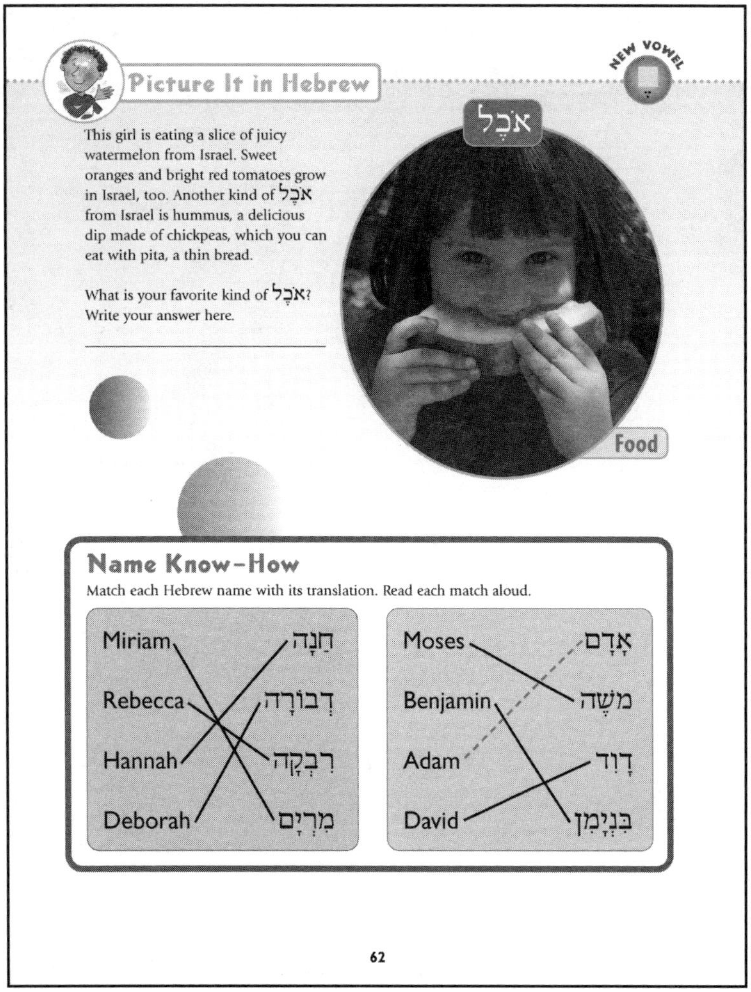

NEW VOWEL

Picture It in Hebrew

אֹכֶל

This girl is eating a slice of juicy watermelon from Israel. Sweet oranges and bright red tomatoes grow in Israel, too. Another kind of אֹכֶל from Israel is hummus, a delicious dip made of chickpeas, which you can eat with pita, a thin bread.

What is your favorite kind of אֹכֶל? Write your answer here.

Food

Name Know-How

Match each Hebrew name with its translation. Read each match aloud.

Miriam	חַנָּה	Moses	אָדָם
Rebecca	דְּבוֹרָה	Benjamin	מֹשֶׁה
Hannah	רִבְקָה	Adam	דָּוִד
Deborah	מִרְיָם	David	בִּנְיָמִן

62

PICTURE IT IN HEBREW

Students have learned all the letters and vowels in the word אֹכֶל and should be encouraged to read it. Test students' knowledge of the individual letters and vowels in the word. First call on students to name each letter. Then have a student pronounce each sound. Finally, have the class read the word together.

Call on a student to read the activity. In turn, have students name their favorite אֹכֶל.

NAME KNOW-HOW

Each Hebrew name represents a biblical figure. Ask if the students can identify any of the people.

Moses – led the Israelites out of Egypt
Benjamin – youngest son of Jacob
Adam – first human being
David – second king of Israel
Miriam – Moses' sister
Rebecca – Isaac's wife
Hannah – mother of the prophet Samuel
Deborah – prophet

ONLINE WORKBOOK

Assign activities from the online workbook and track your students' progress.

LESSON 17

Pages: 63–66
Key Word: פֶּסַח
New Letters: ס פּ
Alef-Bet Flashcards: 34, 35
Word Cards: 44, 47

REVIEW EXERCISE

Distribute *alef-bet* flashcards #1–34 randomly to students. Class size will determine how many cards each student receives. Tell the students in advance that one of the cards being distributed is a new letter to be learned in this lesson.

Call out the name or sound of a letter or vowel and ask the student with that card to hold it up as it is called. Consider calling out letter/vowel combinations to add complexity to this exercise. For example, when calling the word *shemen*, the students with the *shin*, *mem*, *final nun*, *segol*, and *ḥataf segol* cards would all display them.

KEY WORD (פֶּסַח)

Ask the students what the Hebrew name is for the holiday of Passover. What does *Pesaḥ* mean? **[pass over]** Why does the holiday have this name? **[The angel of death passed over the Israelite homes when God delivered the last plague – the killing of the firstborn.]**

"My favorite part of the *Pesaḥ* seder is ____________."

INTRODUCING THE NEW LETTER – פּ

Point to the *pay* on the *alef-bet* chart and ask the student who has the flashcard with this letter to display it. Teach the letter *pay* and its sound. Give special attention to making sure the students can differentiate between the letters *pay*, *bet*, *tav*, *shin*, *mem*, *kaf*, and *tet*.

Have the students point to the *pay* in the word *Pesaḥ* in their textbooks.

READING PRACTICE

Randomly call on students to read each of these three lines. Remember, these lines can be repeated to give more students a chance to read.

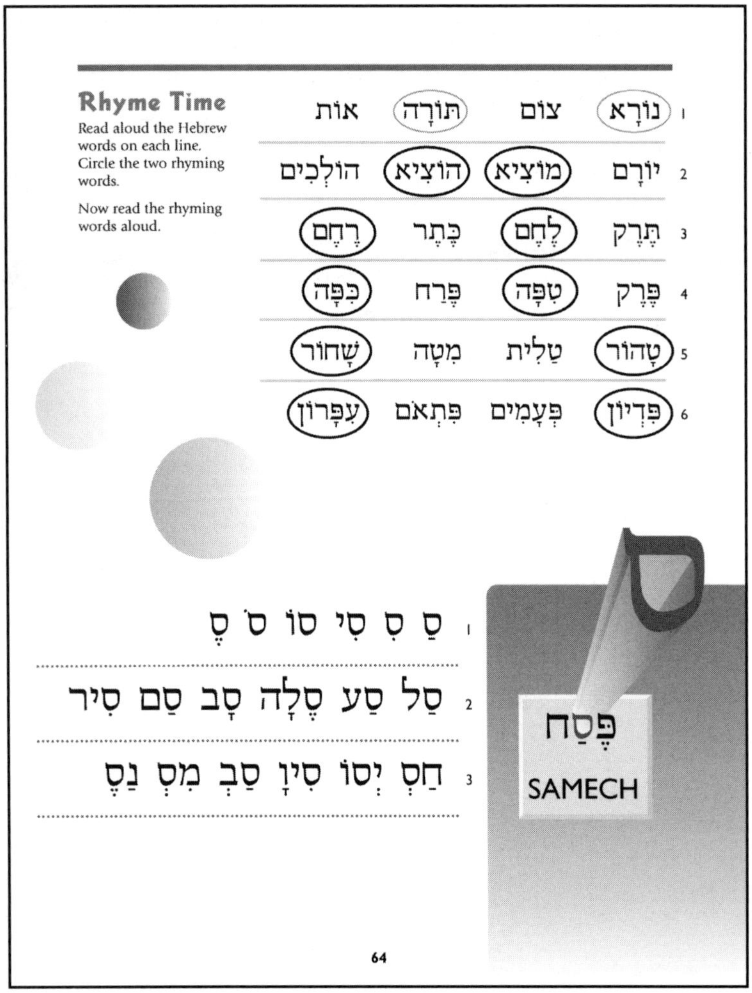

Rhyme Time

Read aloud the Hebrew words on each line. Circle the two rhyming words.

Now read the rhyming words aloud.

1 נוֹרָא צוֹם תּוֹרָה אוֹת

2 יוֹרָם מוֹצִיא הוֹצִיא הוֹלְכִים

3 תֶּרֶק לֶחֶם כֶּתֶר רֶחֶם

4 פֶּרֶק טִפָּה פֶּרַח כִּפָּה

5 טָהוֹר טַלִּית מִטָּה שָׁחוֹר

6 פִּדְיוֹן פְּעָמִים פִּתְאֹם עֶפְרוֹן

ס

1 סַ סְ סִי סוֹ סֹ סֶ

2 סַל סַע סֶלָה סָב סַם סִיר

3 חַס יְסוֹ סִיוָ סַב מִסְ נַסֶ

פֶּסַח

SAMECH

64

RHYME TIME

Have the students complete this exercise independently. Then call on a student to read aloud each of the rhyming sets. Call on another student to read the words on each line that did not rhyme.

Another option is to call on students to come to the chalkboard and write the two words that rhyme. Then have them explain which part of the words are the rhyming sections.

INTRODUCING THE NEW LETTER – ס

Display *alef-bet* flashcard #28 (ם) and ask the students to identify its name and sound. Hold up *alef-bet* flashcard #35 (ס) next to it and have the students describe how the two letters differ. Then teach the *samech's* name and sound. Emphasize that the *samech* is not a final letter.

READING PRACTICE

Read the first line and have the students respond in unison. Call on students to first read line 2 or 3 and to then repeat it singing the sounds to a simple tune.

Ask for a volunteer to read the Key word and to name each of the letters.

NOW READ & READ AGAIN

Number eight slips of paper 1 through 8 and put them in a small bag. When it is each student's turn to read, the student picks a slip of paper out of the bag and reads the line corresponding to the number on the slip. Make sure to recycle the exercise in order to provide reading practice to as many students as possible.

HERITAGE WORDS

What do we do during the *Pesaḥ* seder that shows our חֶסֶד for the Egyptians who enslaved our people? **[take out drops of wine when we recite the ten plagues to show that we cannot be truly happy since people had to suffer and die so that we could be free]**

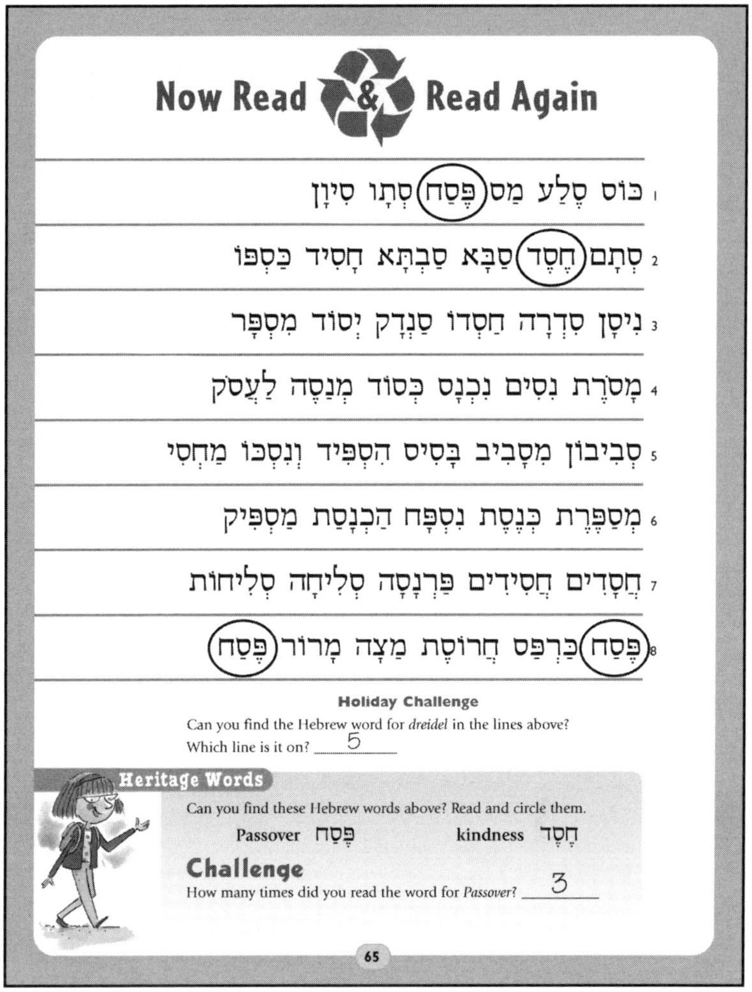

Now Read & Read Again

1 כּוֹס סֶלַע מַס פֶּסַח סְתָו סִיוָן

2 סְתָם חֶסֶד סַבָּא סַבְתָּא חָסִיד כַּסְפּוֹ

3 נִיסָן סִדְרָה חַסְדוֹ סַנְדָּק יְסוֹד מִסְפָּר

4 מָסֹרֶת נִסִּים נִכְנָס כְּסוֹד מְנַסֶּה לַעֲסֹק

5 סְבִיבוֹן מִסָּבִיב בָּסִיס הִסְפִּיד וְנִסְכּוֹ מַחְסִי

6 מְסַפֶּרֶת כְּנֶסֶת נִסְפָּח הַכְנָסַת מַסְפִּיק

7 חֲסָדִים חֲסִידִים פַּרְנָסָה סְלִיחָה סְלִיחוֹת

8 פֶּסַח כַּרְפַּס חֲרוֹסֶת מַצָּה מָרוֹר פֶּסַח

Holiday Challenge

Can you find the Hebrew word for *dreidel* in the lines above?
Which line is it on? 5

Heritage Words

Can you find these Hebrew words above? Read and circle them.

Passover פֶּסַח kindness חֶסֶד

Challenge

How many times did you read the word for *Passover*? 3

65

Picture It in Hebrew

NEW LETTER פ

פִּיצָה

The boy in this photograph is eating פִּיצָה topped with cheese. It is a custom to eat dairy foods, like פִּיצָה, on Shavuot. Some traditional dairy foods for Shavuot are blintzes and noodle pudding. Ice cream is also a dairy food. Which one of these delicious dishes do you like best? Write your answer here.

____

Pizza

Q: How do you fix a broken פִּיצָה?
A: With tomato paste.

The פֶּסַח Seder

Read each Hebrew word and its English meaning aloud. Read each sentence describing a פֶּסַח food. Write the correct word(s) to answer each question.

מָרוֹר	מַצָּה	חֲרוֹסֶת	כַּרְפַּס	יַיִן
bitter herbs	matzah	chopped apples and nuts *ḥaroset*	greens	wine

1 Everyone was in a hurry to leave Egypt and did not have time to wait for the bread dough to rise. My dough hardened into a flat, crunchy kind of bread.

Who am I? matzah מַצָּה

2 I am the greens on the seder plate. I represent springtime and new life. I am dipped into salt water to remind us of the tears we cried when we were slaves.

Who am I? greens כַּרְפַּס

3 I taste bitter. I am a reminder of our bitter lives as slaves. Who am I? bitter herbs מָרוֹר

4 I remind everyone of the bricks we had to make when we were slaves in Egypt.

Who am I? chopped apples and nuts חֲרוֹסֶת

5 I am a sweet liquid. I am poured into a glass four times during the seder. Each of the four times reminds us of God's four promises to bring us from slavery to freedom.

Who am I? wine יַיִן

66

PICTURE IT IN HEBREW

Students have learned all the letters and vowels in the word פִּיצָה and should be encouraged to read it. They'll surely understand what it means!

Ask students: Regular pizza is great on Shavuot, but on Passover, what kind of pizza is better? **[matzah pizza]**

ONLINE WORKBOOK

Assign activities from the online workbook and track your students' progress.

LESSON 18

Pages: 67–69
Key Word: שׁוֹפָר
New Letter: פ
Alef-Bet Flashcard: 36
Word Cards: 48, 49, 50, 51, 52

KEY WORD (שׁוֹפָר)

- What is a shofar and when is it used? **[horn sounded on Rosh Hashanah and Yom Kippur]**
- How do you feel when you hear the sound of the shofar?
- Why do we blow the shofar on Rosh Hashanah? **[reminds us that God is present; an alarm to remind us to pay attention to our lives and our actions; announcement that this day celebrates the creation of the world]**

INTRODUCING THE NEW LETTER – פ

Hold up *alef-bet* flashcard #34 (פּ) and have the students identify the name and sound of the *pay*. Hold up *alef-bet* flashcard #36 (פ) adjacent to #34 and ask the students what is missing. **[the dot in the middle]** Then introduce the *fay* and its sound.

What other letters have almost identical forms? **[בּ-ב, כּ-כ, תּ-ת]**

Direct the students to turn to page 67 and have a volunteer read the Key word at the top of the page.

READING PRACTICE

Read the lines dramatically, as if on stage. For example, have the students read the first line as if they are the giant from Jack and the Beanstalk.

Now Read & Read Again

1 יָפֶה עָפָר כְּפִי נֶפֶשׁ חֹפֶשׁ צוֹפֶה

2 אֹפִי תָּפַס נָפַל אָפָה יָפִים נַפְשִׁי

3 אֹפֶן אֶפֶס צָפוֹן שֶׁפַע כֹּפֶר יִפְתֶּה

4 אָסַפְתָּ אֶפְשָׁר תְּפִלָּה מַפְטִיר תִּפְתַּח לִפְעָמִים

5 תְּפִלּוֹת סְפָרִים סוֹפְרִים לְפָנִים צוֹפִיָּה אַפְקִיד

6 לִפְדּוֹת נוֹפְלִים טוֹטָפֹת נַפְשְׁכֶם תִּפְאֶרֶת

7 אֲפִיקוֹמָן הַפְטָרָה שׁוֹפְטִים כְּמִפְעָלוֹ תְּפִלִּין

8 שׁוֹפָר תְּפִלָּה תְּפִלִּין מַפְטִיר הַפְטָרָה

Heritage Words

Can you find these Hebrew words above? Read and circle them.

prayer תְּפִלָּה shofar שׁוֹפָר
haftarah הַפְטָרָה soul נֶפֶשׁ
afikoman אֲפִיקוֹמָן

Challenge

Can you find the Hebrew word for *haftarah* in the lines above?
Which lines is it on? 7 8
Do you know what the haftarah is? the reading from the book of Prophets after the Torah reading

68

NOW READ & READ AGAIN

Call on students at random to read each of the lines. Keep students on their toes by calling on the same child more than once.

HERITAGE WORDS

נֶפֶשׁ is soul. What is a soul? **[Our souls guide us in the direction of Torah, help us to know right from wrong, and help us use the talents we have to the best of our ability.]** Have students think of two words that they believe describe themselves. For example: loving, talkative, musical, playful, funny, etc. These are all aspects of our soul. Our souls are an important ingredient in who we are and what we do.

It is said that the sound of the שׁוֹפָר awakens our souls. What does this mean? **[The soul serves as our conscience, telling us what is the right way to behave. When we behave wrongly, it may be said that our soul is sleeping. The trumpet sound of the shofar awakens our soul so that we behave in the right and proper way.]**

What is the אֲפִיקוֹמָן? Where in the house have you found the *afikoman*?

תְּפִלָּה is the more general word used to describe the different prayers that we recite. *Brachot* are usually specific blessings recited before or after engaging in a specific action, when asking God for something, or when thanking God.

When is the הַפְטָרָה recited and what is it? **[It is recited after the Torah reading on Shabbat and holidays and consists of selections from the *nevi'im* (Prophets). There is always an aspect of the haftarah that relates to that week's Torah reading.]**

PICTURE IT IN HEBREW

Point to a book on a student's desk and say סֵפֶר. Repeat with a second student. Have students point to a book on their own or a classmate's desk and repeat the word סֵפֶר. Ask: What is the sound in the middle of the word? **[*feh*]**

Challenge: Say to the class: There is one word in the bingo activity at the bottom of the page that has the same letter and vowel in the center of the word. When you have found the word, raise your hand. **[#16, נֶפֶשׁ]** If you know what this word means, keep your hand up. **[soul]** Call on a student who knows the English meaning of the word to read it aloud and give its meaning.

BINGO FOR ONE

Have students complete the activity as directed. Review the activity with the class to ensure that all of the students have the correct English translation for each Hebrew word. Then play Bingo as a class.

Preparation: Write each Hebrew word from the exercise on a small slip of paper. Fold the papers and put them into a box.

Play: Divide the class into two teams. Call a representative of team *alef* to pull a word out of the box and read it aloud. Members of team *alef* put a mark on the corresponding board space in their books. Team *alef*'s representative then returns the word to the box, and team *bet* has a turn. The teams alternate until one team fills a row horizonally, vertically, or diagonally—and wins.

ONLINE WORKBOOK

Assign activities from the online workbook and track your students' progress.

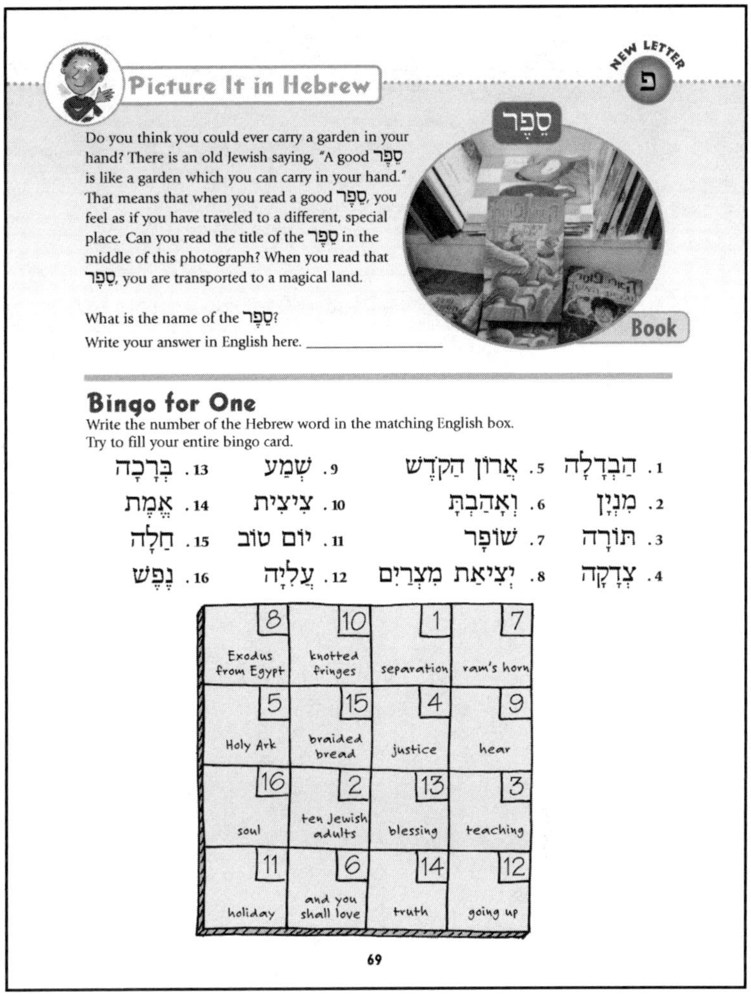
NEW LETTER פ

Picture It in Hebrew

סֵפֶר

Do you think you could ever carry a garden in your hand? There is an old Jewish saying, "A good סֵפֶר is like a garden which you can carry in your hand." That means that when you read a good סֵפֶר, you feel as if you have traveled to a different, special place. Can you read the title of the סֵפֶר in the middle of this photograph? When you read that סֵפֶר, you are transported to a magical land.

Book

What is the name of the סֵפֶר?

Write your answer in English here. ______________

Bingo for One

Write the number of the Hebrew word in the matching English box.
Try to fill your entire bingo card.

1. הַבְדָּלָה
2. מִנְיָן
3. תּוֹרָה
4. צְדָקָה
5. אֲרוֹן הַקֹּדֶשׁ
6. וְאָהַבְתָּ
7. שׁוֹפָר
8. יְצִיאַת מִצְרַיִם
9. שְׁמַע
10. צִיצִית
11. יוֹם טוֹב
12. עֲלִיָּה
13. בְּרָכָה
14. אֱמֶת
15. חַלָּה
16. נֶפֶשׁ

8 Exodus from Egypt	10 knotted fringes	1 separation	7 ram's horn
5 Holy Ark	15 braided bread	4 justice	9 hear
16 soul	2 ten Jewish adults	13 blessing	3 teaching
11 holiday	6 and you shall love	14 truth	12 going up

69

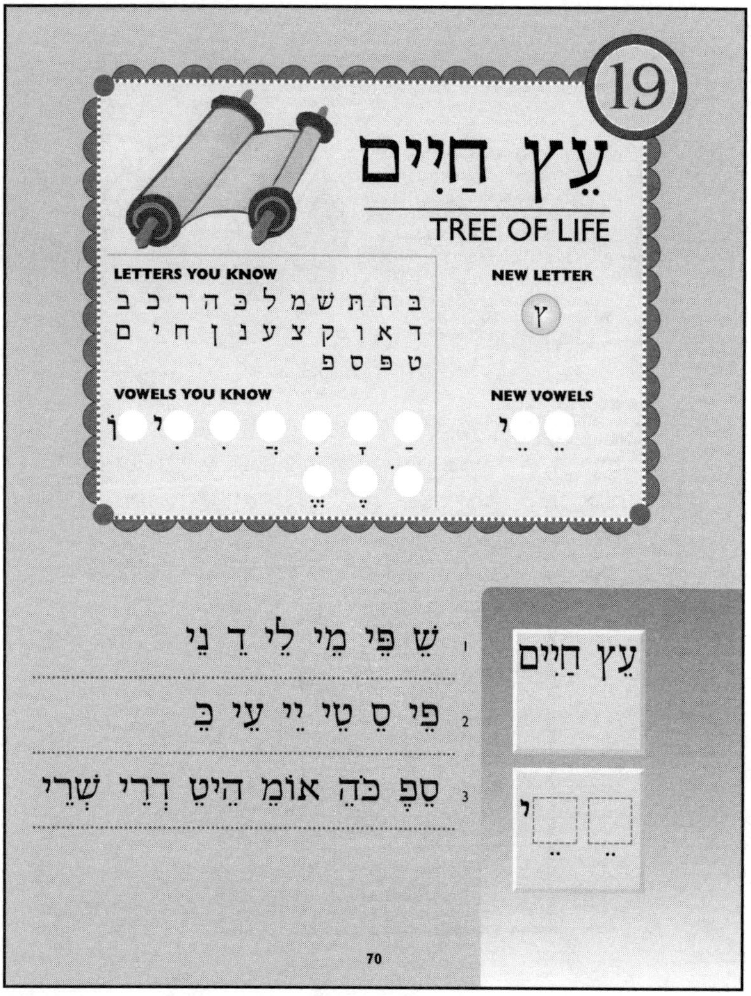
19

עֵץ חַיִּים

TREE OF LIFE

LETTERS YOU KNOW

בּ ת תּ שׁ מ ל כּ ה ר כ ב

ד א ו ק צ ע נ ן ח י ם

ט פּ ס פ

NEW LETTER

ץ

VOWELS YOU KNOW

NEW VOWELS

1 שֵׁ פֵּי מֵי לֵי דֵ נֵי

2 פֵּי סֵ טֵי יֵי עֵי כֵּ

3 סֵפֶ כֹּהֵ אוֹמֵ הֵיטֵ דְרֵי שְׁרֵי

עֵץ חַיִּים

70

LESSON 19

Pages: 70–73
Key Word: עֵץ חַיִּים
New Letter: ץ
New Vowels: ◻ֵ ◻ֵי
Alef-Bet Flashcards: 37, 38, 39
Word Cards: 53, 58

KEY WORD (עֵץ חַיִּים)

Display word card #53 (עֵץ חַיִּים). Ask the students to read the second word. What does it mean? **[life]** Point to the first letter in the first word and ask the students to name it. **[*ayin*]** Read the first word to the students. **[*etz*]** Explain that the word *etz* means "tree."

Students were introduced to the word *l'ḥayyim* in Lesson 13. What does it mean? **[to life]** What does *etz ḥayyim* mean? **[tree of life]**

- Is this phrase from the synagogue service familiar to anyone? **[part of prayer sung when returning the Torah to the Ark at the end of the Torah Service]**
- Why might it be appropriate to sing about *etz ḥayyim* at this point in the service? **[The Torah is our tree of life.]**

Sing Etz Ḥayyim Hee if your students know it.

INTRODUCING THE NEW VOWELS: ◻ֵי ◻ֵ

Using *alef-bet* flashcards #37 and #38, show the new vowel *tsere* to students. Compare it to the vowel *ḥirik*, which has only one dot (*alef-bet* flashcards #21 and #22). Then add the *alef-bet* flashcards for the other vowels learned, review and drill them. (5, 6, 13, 16, 21, 22, 29, 30, 32, 33)

READING PRACTICE

Read line 1 in unison and then call on students individually to read the line. Have one student read line 2 and then have the entire class repeat the line in unison. Do the same with line 3.

RHYME TIME

Ask the students to read aloud the two rhyming words on each line. Challenge the class to find other rhyming words in the eight lines of the exercise. For example, קוֹרֵא – line 3, first word; פִּרְקֵי – line 8, fourth word.

INTRODUCING THE NEW LETTER – ץ

Write the phrase עֵץ חַיִּים on the chalkboard. Call on a student to read the first word aloud. What does it mean? **[tree]** Point to the final *tsadee* in the word and ask which letter looks similar to this. **[*tsadee*]** How do the two letters differ? **[*final tsadee* has a tail]** Hold *alef-bet* flashcards #20 and #39 next to each other. Explain that *alef-bet* flashcard #39 is a *final tsadee.* What two other Hebrew letters learned so far also have a final form? **[*nun* and *mem*]**

Have the class read the entire phrase written on the chalkboard in unison and then call on individuals to read it.

READING PRACTICE

Divide the class into three groups and have each group read one of the three lines in unison. Alternate until each group has read each line.

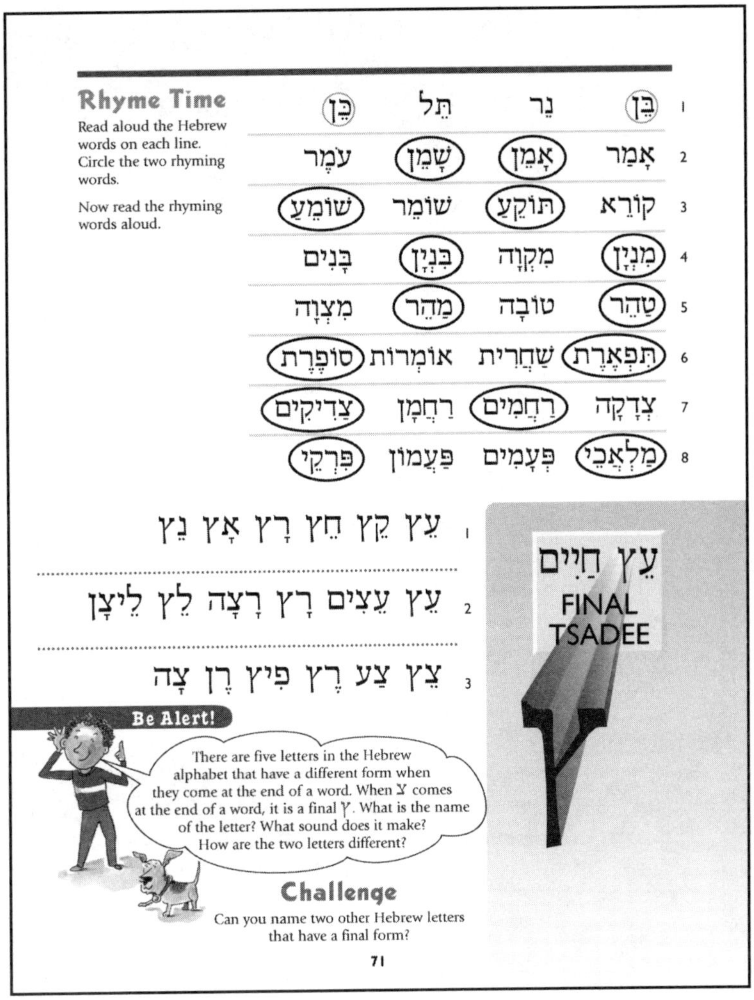

Rhyme Time

Read aloud the Hebrew words on each line. Circle the two rhyming words.

Now read the rhyming words aloud.

1 בֵּן נֵר תֵּל כֵּן

2 אָמַר אָמֵן שָׁמֵן עֹמֶר

3 קוֹרֵא תּוֹקֵעַ שׁוֹמֵר שׁוֹמֵעַ

4 מִנְיָן מִקְוֶה בִּנְיָן בָּנִים

5 טַהֵר טוֹבָה מַהֵר מִצְוָה

6 תִּפְאֶרֶת שַׁחֲרִית אוֹמְרוֹת סוֹפֶרֶת

7 צְדָקָה רַחֲמִים רַחֲמָן צַדִּיקִים

8 מַלְאֲכֵי פְּעָמִים פַּעֲמוֹן פִּרְקֵי

1 עֵץ קֵץ חֵץ רָץ אָץ נֵץ

2 עֵץ עֵצִים רָץ רָצָה לֵץ לֵיצָן

3 צֵץ צַע רֶץ פִּיץ רֶן צָה

Challenge

Can you name two other Hebrew letters that have a final form?

71

Now Read & Read Again

1 אֶרֶץ חָמֵץ מַצָּה חָפֵץ קַיִץ אֹמֶץ

2 קוֹץ קוֹצִים בּוֹץ פָּרַץ קוֹפֵץ קוֹפֶצֶת

3 נוֹצֵץ לוֹחֵץ צַנְחָן עָצִיץ מִיץ נִמְצַץ

4 אִמֵּץ אֶמְצַע מֶרֶץ אָמִיץ הֵצִיץ צִיֵּן

5 לִקְפֹּץ קְפִיצָה קָמַץ חוֹלֵץ חוֹלֵם הֵפִיץ

6 רוֹחֵץ רְחֵצָה יוֹעֵץ צִפֹּרֶן וֶאֱמַץ פֶּרֶץ

7 לְשַׁבֵּץ נִצְטַוָּה מֵלִיץ צְבָעִים צָפוֹן חָמִיץ

8 עֵץ חַיִּים הַמּוֹצִיא לֶחֶם מִן הָאָרֶץ

Heritage Words

Can you find these Hebrew words above? Read and circle them.

tree of life עֵץ חַיִּים leavened food חָמֵץ

Challenge

Can you find the Hebrew word for the special food we eat during פֶּסַח? Underline it.

Can you find the Hebrew word for the food we do not eat on פֶּסַח?

72

NOW READ & READ AGAIN

Call on a student to read the first three words on line 1. Then call on another student to read the next three words until all the words have been read.

When recycling this exercise, ask the students to follow these instructions for each line:

Line #	Instructions
1)	Read the words that contain a *mem*
2)	Read the words that begin with a *kuf*
3)	Read the words that contain a *tsadee*
4)	Read the words that contain a *tsere*
5)	Read the words that contain a final *tsadee*
6)	Read the words that contain a *segol*
7)	Read the words that contain a *ḥirik*
8)	Read the four words that conclude the blessing we recite before eating bread

HERITAGE WORDS

After the students complete the challenge exercise, ask them why we eat matzah and not חָמֵץ on *Pesaḥ*. **[The Israelites' bread dough did not have time to rise when they left Egypt.]**

PICTURE IT IN HEBREW

Students have learned the letters and vowels in the word עֵץ and should be encouraged to read it.

Challenge: Ask: What is the name of the Jewish New Year for the trees? **[Tu B'Shevat]** In what Hebrew month does the holiday fall? **[Shevat]** Who knows what *Tu* stands for? **[ט״ו, 15—the 15th day of the month of Shevat]**

CONNECTIONS

Ask the students if they can translate any of the phrases they completed in this exercise. Some of these words have not yet been taught.

1. *hamotzi leḥem* – who brings forth bread
2. *mah nishtanah* – how is [this night] different
3. *etz ḥayyim* – tree of life
4. *sefer Torah* – Torah scroll
5. *y'tziat mitzrayim* – the Exodus (going out) from Egypt
6. *yom tov* – literally means "good day"; holiday
7. *aron hakodesh* – the holy ark
8. *ner tamid* – eternal light
9. *shana tovah* – literally means "good year;" traditional Rosh Hashanah greeting
10. *shalom aleichem* – peace be with you

ONLINE WORKBOOK

Assign activities from the online workbook and track your students' progress.

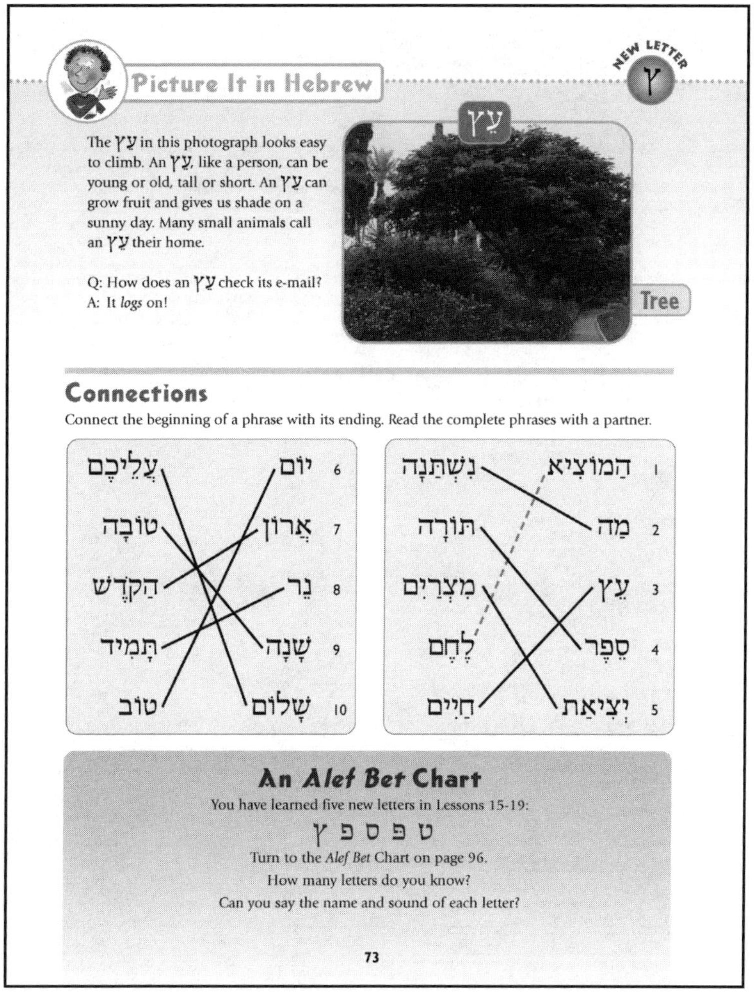

Picture It in Hebrew

NEW LETTER ץ

עֵץ

The עֵץ in this photograph looks easy to climb. An עֵץ, like a person, can be young or old, tall or short. An עֵץ can grow fruit and gives us shade on a sunny day. Many small animals call an עֵץ their home.

Q: How does an עֵץ check its e-mail?
A: It *logs* on!

Tree

Connections

Connect the beginning of a phrase with its ending. Read the complete phrases with a partner.

1 הַמּוֹצִיא — נִשְׁתַּנָּה
2 מַה — תּוֹרָה
3 עֵץ — מִצְרַיִם
4 סֵפֶר — לֶחֶם
5 יְצִיאַת — חַיִּים

6 יוֹם — עֲלֵיכֶם
7 אֲרוֹן — טוֹבָה
8 נֵר — הַקֹּדֶשׁ
9 שָׁנָה — תָּמִיד
10 שָׁלוֹם — טוֹב

An *Alef Bet* Chart

You have learned five new letters in Lessons 15-19:

ט פּ ס פ ץ

Turn to the *Alef Bet* Chart on page 96.
How many letters do you know?
Can you say the name and sound of each letter?

73

20

יִשְׂרָאֵל

ISRAEL

LETTERS YOU KNOW

בּ ת תּ שׁ מ ל כּ ה ר כ ב

ד א ו ק צ ע נ ן ח י ם

ט פּ ס פ ץ

VOWELS YOU KNOW

NEW LETTER

שׂ

1 שָׂ שִׂי שֵׂי שׂוֹ שֶׂ שֵׂ

2 שֵׂ שֶׂ שִׂי שֵׂי שׂוֹ שׂוֹ

3 מַשְׂ שָׂשׂוֹ שֶׂבַ שָׂפָ יִשָׂ עֶשְׂ

יִשְׂרָאֵל

SIN

Be Alert!

The letters שׁ and שׂ make different sounds. What sound does שׁ make? What sound does שׂ make? How do they look different?

74

LESSON 20

Pages: 74–76
Key Word: יִשְׂרָאֵל
New Letter: שׂ
Alef-Bet Flashcard: 40
Word Cards: 59, 60, 61

REVIEW EXERCISE

I Spy

Say, "I spy a *lamed*" or "I spy an '*ah*' sound." Call on a student to come up to the *alef-bet* chart and point to the correct letter or vowel. Next, it is the student's turn to "spy" a letter or vowel. Then have that student call on a classmate to come up and find it.

KEY WORD (יִשְׂרָאֵל)

Display a map of Israel. Ask if anyone knows what country it is. Have any of the students been to Israel? If so, have them share their impressions of the experience.

Why is Israel so important to the Jewish people? **[the Jewish state, birthplace of the Jewish people, etc.]** What do they think it would be like to live in Israel?

INTRODUCING THE NEW LETTER – שׂ

Announce "I spy a *sin*!" and point to the *sin* on the *alef-bet* chart. Hold up word card #59 (יִשְׂרָאֵל), read the word, and point to the *sin*. What sound does the *sin* make? What letter does the *sin* look like? **[*shin*]** How is it different from the *shin*? **[location of the dot]** What other letter has an "s" sound? **[*samech*]**

READING PRACTICE

Randomly call on students to read each of these three lines.

NOW READ & READ AGAIN

Have one student read a line and then have that student call out the name of the next reader.

For further reading practice, continue the "I spy" theme by announcing words at random from the eight lines. For example, "I spy the third word on the second line." Then the student who is called on to read that word should "spy" a new word and select a classmate to recite it.

HERITAGE WORDS

עֲשֶׂרֶת הַדִּבְּרוֹת literally means "the ten sayings" or "the ten utterances." Why were the Ten Commandments given this name? **[the words were said or uttered by God]** What is the Hebrew word for commandments? **[מִצְוֹת]**

Can you list each of the Ten Commandments?

1. God is One and there is no other
2. You shall worship no other gods
3. You shall not speak falsely in God's name
4. Remember the Sabbath day, to keep it holy
5. Honor your father and your mother
6. You shall not murder
7. You shall not be false to your wife or husband
8. You shall not steal
9. You shall not lie
10. You shall not want things that belong to someone else

Have you ever heard someone say that something is a *simḥah*? This means that it is a happy event and comes from the word שָׂמֵחַ, which means "happy."

WORD RIDDLE

Answer: שִׂמְחַת תּוֹרָה

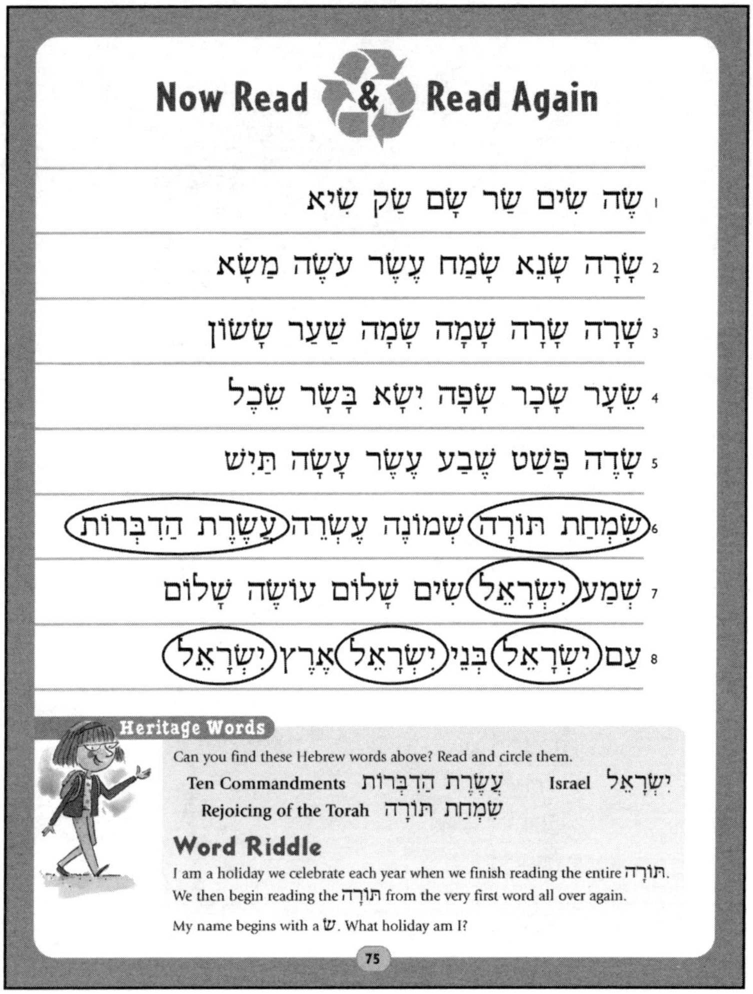

Now Read & Read Again

1 שֶׁה שִׁים שַׁר שָׁם שַׁק שִׂיא
2 שָׂרָה שָׂנֵא שָׂמַח עֶשֶׂר עֹשֶׂה מַשָּׂא
3 שָׂרָה שָׁרָה שָׁמָה שָׂמָה שַׁעַר שָׂשׂוֹן
4 שֵׂעָר שָׂכָר שָׂפָה יִשָּׂא בָּשָׂר שֵׂכֶל
5 שָׂדֶה פָּשַׁט שֶׁבַע עֶשֶׂר עָשָׂה תַּיִשׁ
6 שִׂמְחַת תּוֹרָה שְׁמוֹנֶה עֶשְׂרֵה עֲשֶׂרֶת הַדִּבְּרוֹת
7 שְׁמַע יִשְׂרָאֵל שִׂים שָׁלוֹם עוֹשֶׂה שָׁלוֹם
8 עַם יִשְׂרָאֵל בְּנֵי יִשְׂרָאֵל אֶרֶץ יִשְׂרָאֵל

Heritage Words

Can you find these Hebrew words above? Read and circle them.

Ten Commandments עֲשֶׂרֶת הַדִּבְּרוֹת — Israel יִשְׂרָאֵל

Rejoicing of the Torah שִׂמְחַת תּוֹרָה

Word Riddle

I am a holiday we celebrate each year when we finish reading the entire תּוֹרָה. We then begin reading the תּוֹרָה from the very first word all over again.

My name begins with a שׂ. What holiday am I?

75

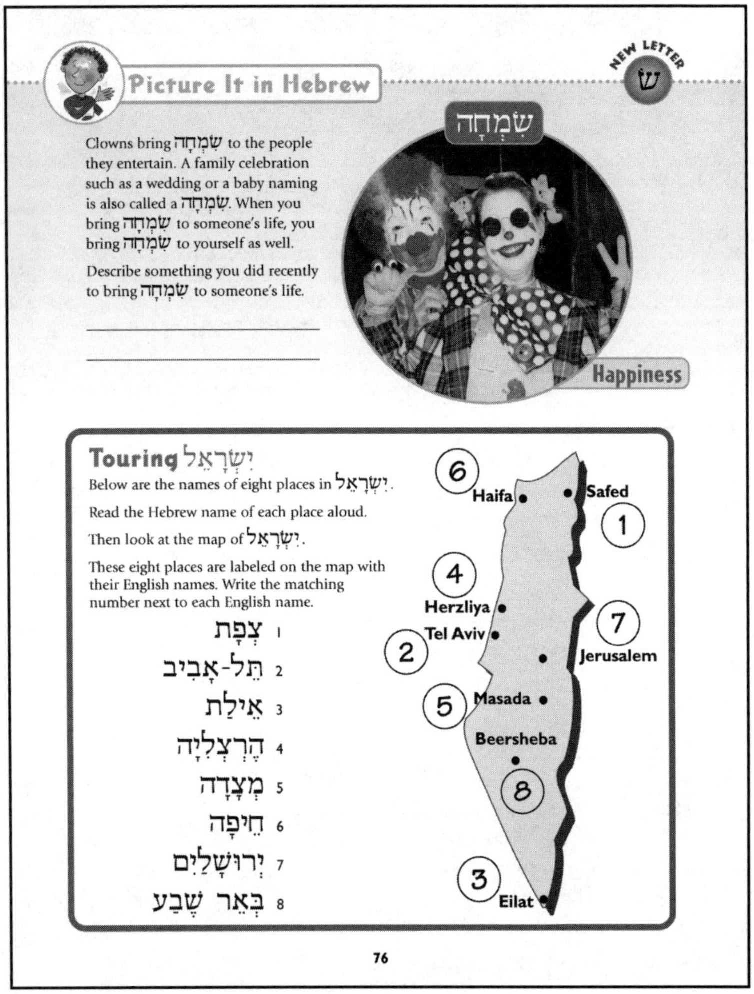

PICTURE IT IN HEBREW

Students have learned all the letters and vowels in the word שִׂמְחָה and should be encouraged to read it.
Ask students to identify all the letters and vowels—and their sounds—in the word שִׂמְחָה.

Ask students who have recently celebrated a שִׂמְחָה to describe the event.

TOURING יִשְׂרָאֵל

1. Safed
2. Tel Aviv
3. Eilat
4. Herzliya
5. Masada
6. Haifa
7. Jerusalem
8. Beersheba

ONLINE WORKBOOK

Assign activities from the online workbook and track your students' progress.

LESSON 21

Pages: 77–80
Key Word: חַג שָׂמֵחַ
New Letter: ג
Alef-Bet Flashcard: 41
Word Cards: 62, 66

KEY WORD (חַג שָׂמֵחַ)

Display word card #62 (חַג שָׂמֵחַ) and have the students read the second word. What does *same'aḥ* mean? **[happy]** Read the entire phrase and define it. **[traditional holiday greeting – "happy holiday"]** Have the students list occasions when you might wish someone a *ḥag same'aḥ*. **[Simḥat Torah, Sukkot, Pesaḥ, etc.]** Have the students practice saying *ḥag same'aḥ* to one another.

INTRODUCING THE NEW LETTER – ג

Print the word סְבִיבוֹן on the chalkboard and ask the students to read and identify the word. **[dreidel]** What letters are on a *s'vivon*? **[נ ג ה שׁ]** Although the students have not formally learned the *gimmel* yet, they may be familiar with it from the dreidel game. Point to the *gimmel* on the *alef-bet* chart and on word card #62. Formally teach the *gimmel* to the class. Next, point to the *nun* on the *alef-bet* chart. How do the *gimmel* and *nun* differ in appearance?

READING PRACTICE

Continuing with the *s'vivon* theme, write on the chalkboard the rules for the *Shalom Uvrachah Primer Express* version of the dreidel game.

Gimmel	–	read no lines
Nun	–	read line 1
Hay	–	read lines 1 and 2
Shin	–	read lines 1, 2, and 3

Each student, in turn, spins a dreidel and then follows the rules above.

1 כֹּחַ מֹחַ רֵיחַ נֹחַ שִׂיחַ אֹחַ

2 יָרֵחַ בְּכֹּחַ הַמֹּחַ לְנֹחַ כְּשִׂיחַ טִיחַ

3 רֵחַ מִיחַ שִׂיחַ גִיחַ רֹחַ נוֹחַ

Making Faces

In each circle below draw a face (eyes, eyebrows, nose, mouth, ears, hair) to reflect the emotion indicated by the Hebrew and English words.

בַּיְשָׁן	עַקְשָׁן	פַּחְדָן	נִרְגָּשׁ	כּוֹעֵס	שָׂמֵחַ
bashful	stubborn	fearful	excited	angry	happy

Be Alert!

When חַ comes at the end of a word, the vowel is read first and then the letter. It sounds like אַח. (שָׂמֵחַ = שָׂמֵאַח)

78

READING PRACTICE

Have the students look at the Key word and point to the *ḥet* at the end of *same'aḥ*. Explain the special rule that applies in these cases, as noted in the Be Alert section. Call on students to read the entire phrase.

Have students randomly read words from these three lines. Emphasize the "ḥ" sound.

MAKING FACES

After the students have completed the exercise, play "Making Faces Charades." Call a "contestant" to the front of the room. Point to the emotion in the book that the student should portray so that no one else can see it. As the student acts out the emotion, classmates raise their hands to guess which it is. Call on a student to read the answer from the book. If it is correct, that student is the next contestant.

NOW READ & READ AGAIN

Call on students to read a line of text aloud. For a change of pace, first read all the odd-numbered lines followed by the even-numbered lines.

HERITAGE WORDS

What do we believe will happen when the מָשִׁיחַ comes? **[There will be peace in the world.]** According to our tradition, who will anounce that the Messiah is about to come? **[Elijah the Prophet]** When do we sing the song *Eliyahu Hanavi*, about our hope that Elijah will come soon to announce the coming of the Messiah? **[*Havdalah* at the end of Shabbat; during the *Pesaḥ* seder.]**

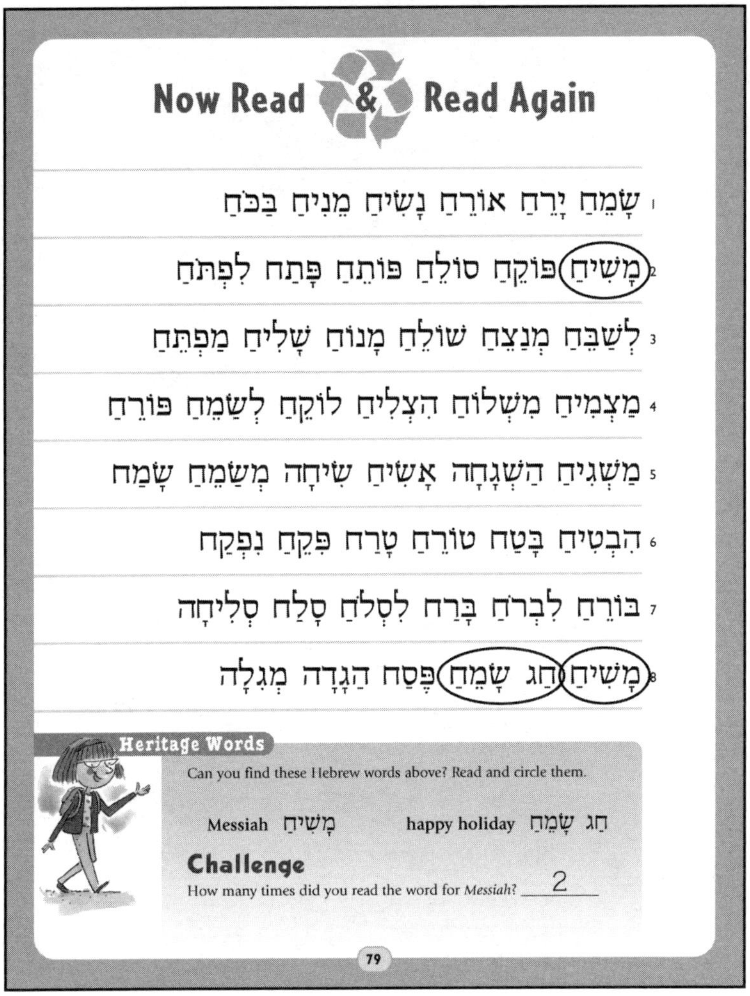

Now Read & Read Again

1 שָׂמֵחַ יָרֵחַ אוֹרֵחַ נָשִׂיחַ מֵנִיחַ בַּכֹּחַ

2 מָשִׁיחַ פּוֹקֵחַ סוֹלֵחַ פּוֹתֵחַ פָּתַח לִפְתֹּחַ

3 לְשַׁבֵּחַ מְנַצֵּחַ שׁוֹלֵחַ מָנוֹחַ שָׁלִיחַ מַפְתֵּחַ

4 מַצְמִיחַ מִשְׁלוֹחַ הִצְלִיחַ לוֹקֵחַ לְשַׂמֵּחַ פּוֹרֵחַ

5 מַשְׁגִּיחַ הַשְׁגָּחָה אָשִׂיחַ שִׂיחָה מְשַׂמֵּחַ שָׂמַח

6 הִבְטִיחַ בָּטַח טוֹרֵחַ טָרַח פִּקֵּחַ נִפְקַח

7 בּוֹרֵחַ לִבְרֹחַ בָּרַח לִסְלֹחַ סָלַח סְלִיחָה

8 מָשִׁיחַ חַג שָׂמֵחַ פֶּסַח הַגָּדָה מְגִלָּה

Heritage Words

Can you find these Hebrew words above? Read and circle them.

Messiah מָשִׁיחַ happy holiday חַג שָׂמֵחַ

Challenge

How many times did you read the word for *Messiah*? 2

79

Picture It in Hebrew

NEW LETTER ג

This tired גָּמָל is resting by the side of a road. A גָּמָל can travel great distances across hot, dry deserts with little food or water. The גָּמָל walks easily on soft sand where trucks would get stuck, and carries people and heavy loads to places that have no roads. A גָּמָל carries its own built-in food supply on its back—its hump! If the גָּמָל doesn't eat for a long time, its hump becomes small.

גָּמָל

Camel

Q: What does a גָּמָל wear when it wants to hide?
A: Camel-flage!

I Have a Little Dreidel

Add the ending sound חַ to complete each word on the dreidels. Read the words to a classmate.

לְהָנִיחַ מִטְבֵּחַ מְשַׂמֵּחַ סוֹלֵחַ

הַמְנַבֵּחַ שׁוֹלֵחַ לְשַׁבֵּחַ

80

PICTURE IT IN HEBREW

Students have learned all the letters and vowels in the word גָּמָל and should be encouraged to read it.

Call on individual students to read the paragraphs. Ask if anyone in the class has ever ridden a גָּמָל and, if so, to describe the experience.

I HAVE A LITTLE DREIDEL

Have students complete the activity as directed. For added practice, play "Dreidel Spin-Off" with the class. Bring in dreidels. Divide the class into pairs and give each pair a dreidel. Students take turns spinning the dreidel. When the dreidel stops, the student reads an assigned word from the exercise. If the word is correct, the student earns a point. If incorrect, the student loses a point. Continue until both students in every pair have read all the words.

ONLINE WORKBOOK

Assign activities from the online workbook and track your students' progress.

LESSON 22

Pages: 81–84
Key Word: קִדּוּשׁ
New Vowels: וּ ◌ֻ
Alef-Bet Flashcards: 42, 43
Word Cards: 67, 68, 69, 70, 71, 72

KEY WORD (קִדּוּשׁ)

On Shabbat and on a *ḥag* we fulfill the mitzvah of declaring the day holy by reciting which prayer over wine or grape juice? **[Kiddush]**

What does it mean to be holy? **[being special, different, unique, etc.]**

Have the students complete the following sentence: "I feel holy when ______________."

INTRODUCING NEW VOWELS – (SHURUK: וּ and KUBUTZ: ◌ֻ)

Display *alef-bet* flashcard #42 (וּ) and introduce its sound to the students. Then display *alef-bet* flashcards #18 (ו) and #29 (וֹ). Have the students identify these two cards and describe how they differ from the *shuruk*.

Hold up *alef-bet* flashcard #43 (◌ֻ) next to *alef-bet* flash card #42 (וּ) and explain that both have the same sound. What other vowels are similar in appearance to the *kubutz* and in what way do they differ? **[*segol*, *shvah*, *tsere*, *ḥirik* – number and/or configuration of dots]**

Display word cards #19 (קַדִּישׁ – Kaddish), #35 (קָדוֹשׁ – holy), and #67 (קִדּוּשׁ – Kiddush). Have the students read and define each of these words. What is similar in each of these words? **[קדשׁ – the root letters meaning "holy"]**

READING PRACTICE

Randomly call on individuals to read each of the three lines.

Now Read & Read Again

1 חֻמָּשׁ לוּחַ כֻּלָּם וְהָיוּ סֻכָּה טֹבוּ

2 עָלֵינוּ לְבֵנוּ סֻכּוֹת שָׁבוּעַ חֲנֻכָּה קִבּוּץ

3 קִדּוּשׁ שֻׁלְחָן מְשֻׁבָּח סִדּוּר מְצֻיָּן כֻּלָּנוּ

4 הַלְלוּיָה גְדֻלָּה פָּסוּק יְשׁוּעָה נְטוּיָה אֲנַחְנוּ

5 וּבְנֻחָה לוּלָב וְיָפֻצוּ וַיְכֻלוּ וְיָנֻסוּ דַיֵּנוּ

6 תְּמוּנָה וְצִוָּנוּ אֵלִיָּהוּ הַנָּבִיא בָּרְכוּ קֻשְׁיוֹת

7 קְדֻשָּׁה יְהוּדִים פּוּרִים יוֹם כִּפּוּר שָׁבוּעוֹת

8 יְרוּשָׁלַיִם אֱלֹהֵינוּ שֶׁהֶחֱיָנוּ אָבִינוּ מַלְכֵּנוּ

Heritage Words

Can you find these Hebrew words above? Read and circle them.

The Five Books of Moses	חֻמָּשׁ	Kiddush	קִדּוּשׁ
Jerusalem	יְרוּשָׁלַיִם	prayerbook	סִדּוּר
Elijah the prophet	אֵלִיָּהוּ הַנָּבִיא	Jews	יְהוּדִים

Challenge

Can you find the Hebrew word for *prayerbook* in the lines above? Underline the word.

82

NOW READ & READ AGAIN

Call on students at random to read lines 1–8.

HERITAGE WORDS

Another name for the Torah is חֻמָּשׁ. The word *ḥumash* comes from the word *ḥamesh* (five) and refers to the fact that the Torah comprises five books. What are the five books of the Torah? **[Genesis – *Bereshit*, Exodus – *Shemot*, Leviticus –*Vayikra*, Numbers – *Bemidbar*, Deuteronomy – *Devarim*]**

What is the capital of Israel? **[יְרוּשָׁלַיִם]**

Who is supposed to announce that the Messiah will be coming? **[אֵלִיָּהוּ הַנָּבִיא]**

POWER READING

Call on students to read each of these six phrases from the Shabbat Evening Kiddush. Afterwards, the teacher should sing or read aloud the full text of the Kiddush. As each phrase in the textbook is recited, the students should raise their hands. Pause, compliment the students, tell them to lower their hands, and then continue. Repeat this procedure until the end of the Kiddush.

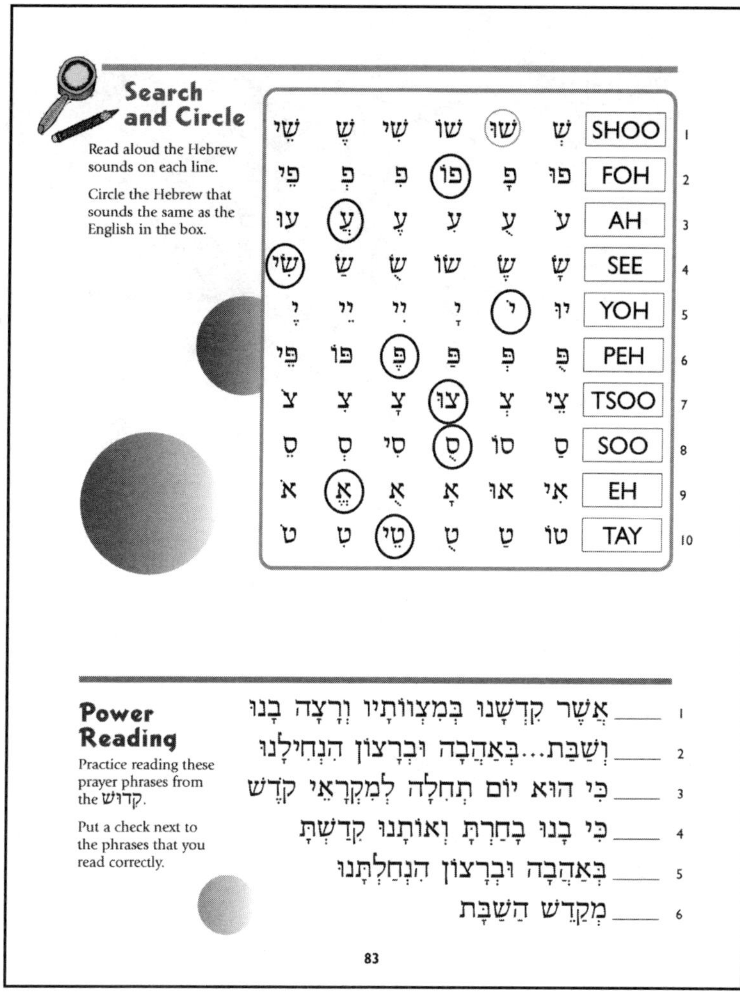

Search and Circle

Read aloud the Hebrew sounds on each line.

Circle the Hebrew that sounds the same as the English in the box.

1	SHOO	שֻׁ	שׁוּ	שׁוֹ	שִׁי	שֶׁ	שֵׁי
2	FOH	פוּ	פָ	פוֹ	פִ	פְ	פֵי
3	AH	עֹ	עֱ	עֶ	עִ	עֶ	עֲ	עוּ
4	SEE	שָׁ	שֶׁ	שׁוּ	שֱ	שַׁ	שִׁי
5	YOH	יוּ	יֹ	יָ	יִי	יֵי	יֵ
6	PEH	פֱּ	פְּ	פַּ	פֶּ	פּוֹ	פֵּי
7	TSOO	צֵי	צְ	צוּ	צָ	צִ	צֹ
8	SOO	סֵ	סוֹ	סֻ	סִי	סְ	סֵ
9	EH	אִי	אוּ	אָ	אֱ	אֱ	אֹ
10	TAY	טוֹ	טַ	טֱ	טֵי	טִ	טֹ

Power Reading

Practice reading these prayer phrases from the קִדּוּשׁ.

Put a check next to the phrases that you read correctly.

1 ____ אֲשֶׁר קִדְּשָׁנוּ בְּמִצְווֹתָיו וְרָצָה בָנוּ

2 ____ וְשַׁבַּת...בְּאַהֲבָה וּבְרָצוֹן הִנְחִילָנוּ

3 ____ כִּי הוּא יוֹם תְּחִלָּה לְמִקְרָאֵי קֹדֶשׁ

4 ____ כִּי בָנוּ בָחַרְתָּ וְאוֹתָנוּ קִדַּשְׁתָּ

5 ____ בְּאַהֲבָה וּבְרָצוֹן הִנְחַלְתָּנוּ

6 ____ מְקַדֵּשׁ הַשַּׁבָּת

83

Picture It in Hebrew

NEW VOWEL וּ

How would you like to eat a קַקְטוּס? A קַקְטוּס plant is covered with prickly spines, but if you pick carefully, you can use some kinds of קַקְטוּס for food. Jams and sweets are made from their fruits and juicy stems. Sometimes a קַקְטוּס, like the one you see in this photograph, looks like a pipe or a tree. A person born in Israel is sometimes called a *Sabra,* which is a kind of prickly-pear קַקְטוּס that grows in Israel. Like the *Sabra,* some Israelis can be prickly on the outside but sweet on the inside.

קַקְטוּס

Cactus

Holiday Quiz

Draw a line from each holiday in the right-hand column to its matching explanation in the left-hand column.

1 We read the מְגִלָּה.	יוֹם כִּפּוּר
2 We shake the lulav and eat in a small booth.	פּוּרִים
3 We celebrate the Giving of the Torah.	סֻכּוֹת
4 We light the *ḥanukkiah*.	שָׁבוּעוֹת
5 We do not eat all day.	חֲנֻכָּה

84

PICTURE IT IN HEBREW

By now, students should be able to read almost all of the "Picture It in Hebrew" words. The cognate קַקְטוּס is no exception. Have students read the word several times. Then review all the letters and vowels in the word. Ask if anyone in the class has eaten a cactus and, if so, to describe the experience.

Enrichment: If you have a cactus plant at home, bring it in to illustrate the word קַקְטוּס. Students will never forget it!

ONLINE WORKBOOK

Assign activities from the online workbook and track your students' progress.

LESSON 23

Pages: 85–88
Key Word: מְזוּזָה
New Letter: ז
Alef-Bet Flashcard: 44
Word Cards: 73, 74, 75

REVIEW EXERCISE

Basketball

Drill the students on *alef-bet* flashcards 1–43 using a basketball theme. Divide the class into two teams. Each correct answer is worth two points. An incorrect answer moves the turn to the other team.

KEY WORD (מְזוּזָה)

If the doorpost to your classroom has a *mezuzah*, ask a student to point it out.

- What is inside a *mezuzah*? **[piece of parchment with the Shema written on it]**
- Why do we hang a *mezuzah*? **[The Shema tells us to love God, to keep God's commandments, and to put God's words on our doorposts.]**
- What do many Jews do when entering a room with a *mezuzah*? **[kiss the *mezuzah*]**

INTRODUCING THE NEW LETTER – ז

Print the following letters on the chalkboard and review them:

ו ן וֹ וּ

Print a *zayin* on the chalkboard and introduce this new letter. How does the *zayin* differ in appearance from the other letters on the chalkboard? Display word card #73 and have a student point out the two *zayins* and then read the word.

READING PRACTICE

Return to the "basketball theme," calling on individuals to read each of the three lines and then having their teammates repeat them in unison.

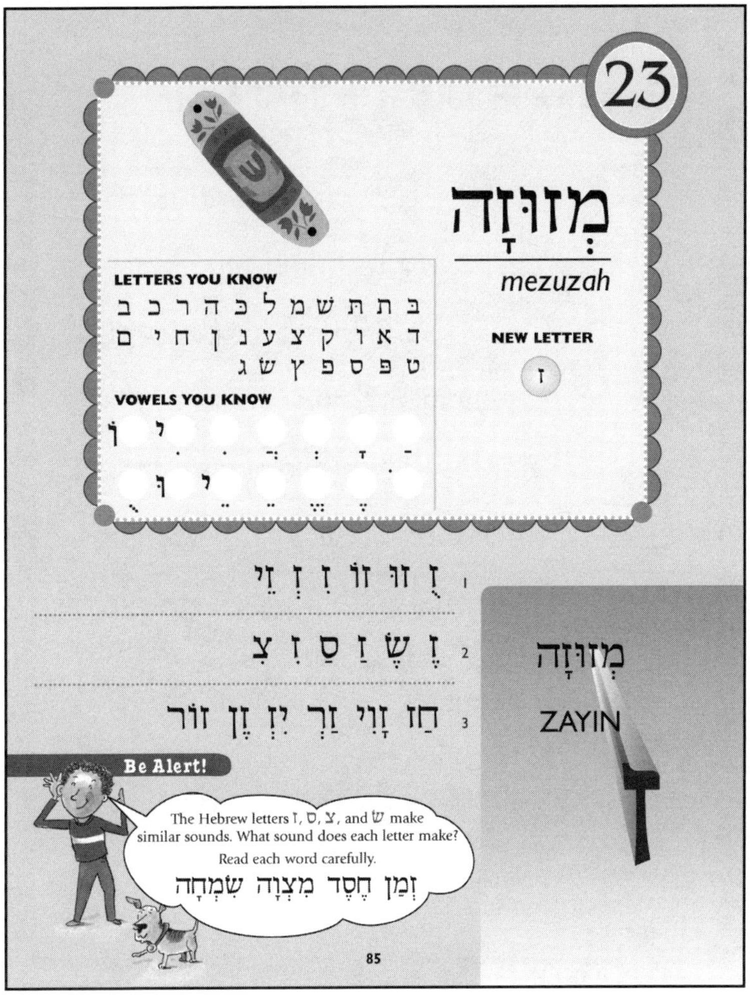

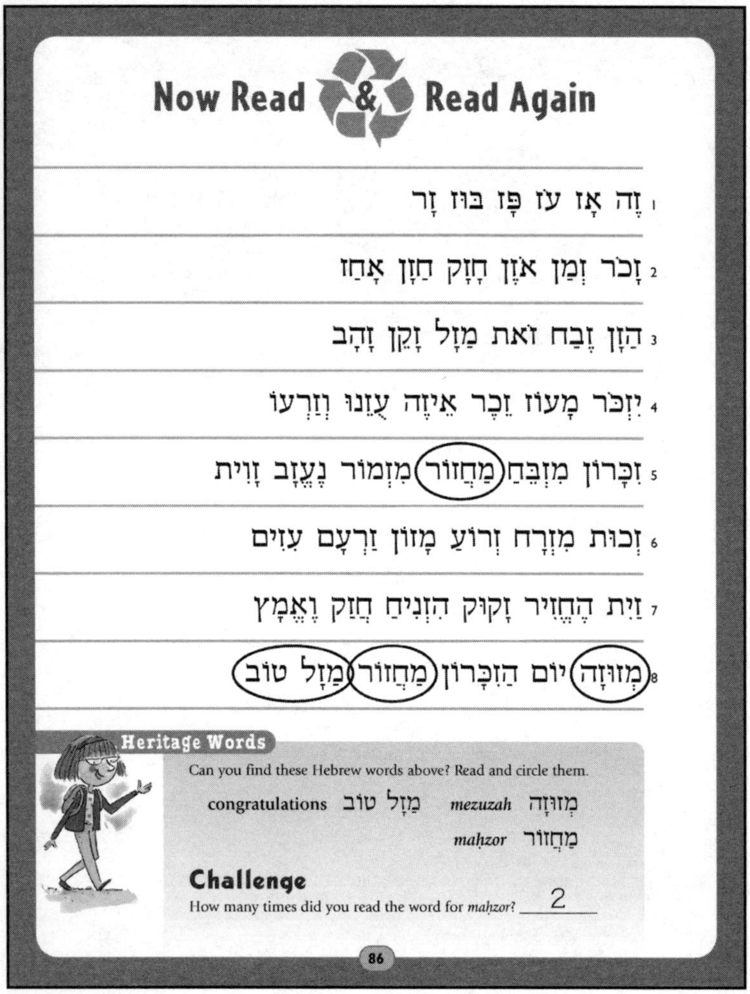

Now Read & Read Again

1 זֶה אָז עֹז פָּז בּוּז זָר

2 זָכֹר זְמַן אֹזֶן חָזָק חַזָן אָחַז

3 הַזָן זֶבַח זֹאת מַזָל זָקֵן זָהָב

4 יִזְכֹּר מָעוֹז זֵכֶר אֵיזֶה עֲזֵנוּ וְזַרְעוֹ

5 זִכָּרוֹן מִזְבֵּחַ מַחֲזוֹר מִזְמוֹר נֶעֱזָב זָוִית

6 זְכוּת מִזְרָח זְרוֹעַ מָזוֹן זַרְעָם עִזִים

7 זַיִת הֶחֱזִיר זָקוּק הִזְנִיחַ חֲזַק וֶאֱמָץ

8 מְזוּזָה יוֹם הַזִכָּרוֹן מַחֲזוֹר מַזָל טוֹב

Heritage Words

Can you find these Hebrew words above? Read and circle them.

congratulations מַזָל טוֹב   *mezuzah* מְזוּזָה

maḥzor מַחֲזוֹר

Challenge

How many times did you read the word for *maḥzor*? 2

86

NOW READ & READ AGAIN

Call out a specific word, such as "line 3, fourth word," and have a student read that word. Have the student call out the next one, or continue to call them out yourself.

HERITAGE WORDS

On what occasions might it be appropriate to wish someone מַזָל טוֹב?

What is a מַחֲזוֹר and on what holidays do we use a it? **[prayer book used on Rosh Hashanah and Yom Kippur]**

SEARCH AND CIRCLE

Have the students complete this exercise independently. Call on students at random to read each line aloud and to identify the Hebrew letter that should be circled.

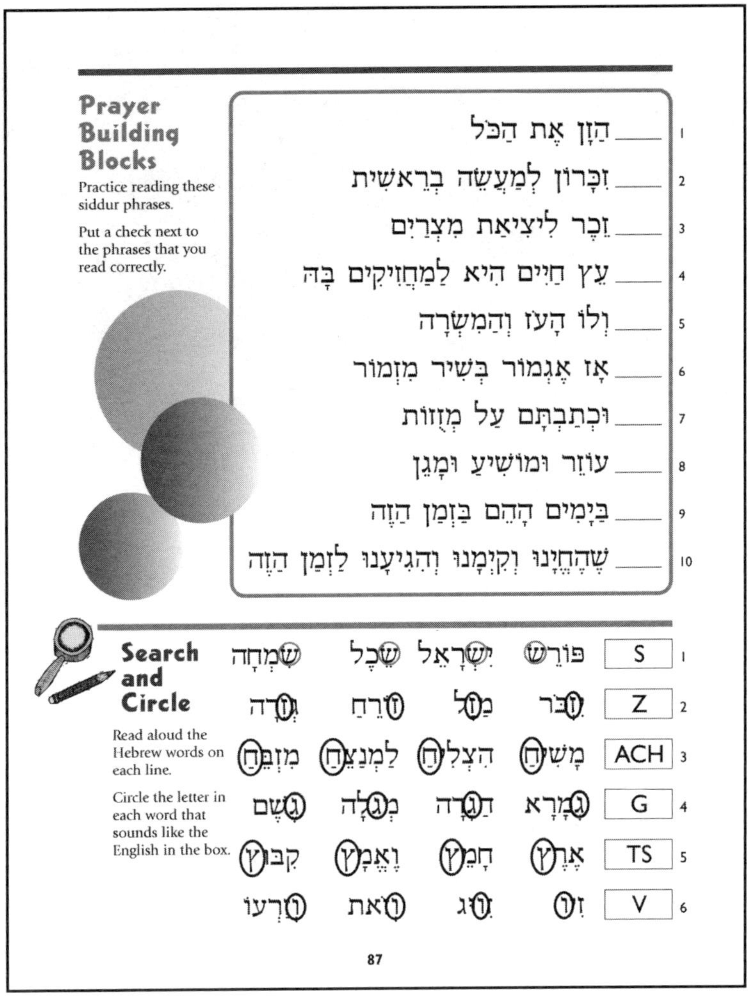

Prayer Building Blocks

Practice reading these siddur phrases.

Put a check next to the phrases that you read correctly.

1 ___ הַזָּן אֶת הַכֹּל
2 ___ זִכָּרוֹן לְמַעֲשֵׂה בְרֵאשִׁית
3 ___ זֵכֶר לִיצִיאַת מִצְרָיִם
4 ___ עֵץ חַיִּים הִיא לַמַּחֲזִיקִים בָּהּ
5 ___ וְלוֹ הָעֹז וְהַמִּשְׂרָה
6 ___ אָז אֶגְמוֹר בְּשִׁיר מִזְמוֹר
7 ___ וּכְתַבְתָּם עַל מְזֻזוֹת
8 ___ עוֹזֵר וּמוֹשִׁיעַ וּמָגֵן
9 ___ בַּיָּמִים הָהֵם בַּזְּמַן הַזֶּה
10 ___ שֶׁהֶחֱיָנוּ וְקִיְּמָנוּ וְהִגִּיעָנוּ לַזְּמַן הַזֶּה

Search and Circle

Read aloud the Hebrew words on each line.

Circle the letter in each word that sounds like the English in the box.

1 S — פּוֹרֵשׁ יִשְׂרָאֵל שֵׂכֶל שִׂמְחָה
2 Z — זָכַר מַזָּל זוֹרֵחַ גִּזְרָה
3 ACH — מָשִׁיחַ הִצְלִיחַ לַמְנַצֵּחַ מִזְבֵּחַ
4 G — גְּמָרָא הַגָּדָה מְגִלָּה גֶּשֶׁם
5 TS — אֶרֶץ חָמֵץ וְאֶמֶץ קִבּוּץ
6 V — זִו וָג וֹאת וֹרְעוּ

87

NEW LETTER ז

Picture It in Hebrew

Looking at this photograph you can see one reason why Jerusalem is often called "Jerusalem of זָהָב." In the center you see the Dome of the Rock mosque, which was built during the seventh century. It has a large, gleaming dome of זָהָב. Bright sun shines on the stone buildings around it, making them glow זָהָב too.

Hebrew Math

Hebrew letters stand for numbers.

5 = ה	4 = ד	3 = ג	2 = ב	1 = א
10 = י	9 = ט	8 = ח	7 = ז	6 = ו

Can you solve these math problems?
Have a classmate check your work.

10 = ה + ה .3	4 = ג − ז .2	3 = ב + א .1
2 = ז − ט .6	10 = ד + ו .5	18 = ח + י .4
6 = ד − י .9	13 = י + ג .8	2 = ו − ח .7
8 = ג + ה .12	10 = א + ט .11	14 = ז + ז .10

88

PICTURE IT IN HEBREW

Read the word זָהָב with the class. Explain that they can see the Dome of the Rock in Jerusalem, the city of זָהָב.

Ask if anyone in the class is wearing something made of זָהָב. If so, have the student(s) stand and point to the item while saying the word זָהָב.

Enrichment: Play *Yerushalayim Shel Zahav* by Naomi Shemer, and tell the students a brief history of the song:

The Israeli government commissioned Naomi Shemer to write a song for the National Song Festival in May 1967, several weeks before the Six-Day War began. Before the Six-Day War, Jerusalem was divided, with the eastern section of the city in Jordanian hands. The beginning of the song tells about the sadness Israelis felt because Jerusalem was divided. The last verse, which Shemer added after the war in 1967, expresses joy that the city was at last reunited.

Have the class listen carefully to the song and raise their hands every time they hear the word זָהָב.

HEBREW MATH

Have students complete the activity as directed. Then invite them to make up their own math problems and test their classmates.

ONLINE WORKBOOK

Assign activities from the online workbook and track your students' progress.

LESSON 24

Pages: 89–91
Key Word: בָּרוּךְ
New Letter: ך
Alef-Bet Flashcard: 45
Word Cards: 76, 77

KEY WORD (בָּרוּךְ)

Hold up word card #6 (בְּרָכָה). Have a volunteer read and define it. Ask what word begins most *brachot*. **[בָּרוּךְ]** Display word card #76.

Have students name *brachot* that begin with the word *baruch.*

INTRODUCING THE NEW LETTER – ך

Have the students look at the *alef-bet* chart and identify all the letters they have learned that have a "partner" or family letter that is a final letter. **[מ צ נ]** Point to the *final chaf* and introduce it. As with the *chaf* and *ḥet*, you may have to emphasize the "*ch*" sound.

How does the final *chaf* differ in appearance from the *dalet* and *final nun?*

READING PRACTICE

Have the students look at the Key word in the textbook and ask a volunteer to read and define it.

Read line 1 in unison and then call on students individually to read the line. Have one student read line 2 and then have the entire class repeat the line in unison.

24
בָּרוּךְ
PRAISED, BLESSED

LETTERS YOU KNOW
בּ תּ ת שׁ מ ל כּ ה ר כ ב
ד א ו ק צ ע נ ן ח י ם
ט פּ ס פ ץ שׂ ג ז

VOWELS YOU KNOW

NEW LETTER
ךְ

1 רַךְ כַּךְ בָּךְ לֵךְ לָךְ וּלְךָ

2 אַךְ בְּךָ שֶׁלְךָ בְּכָךְ שִׁמְךָ תֶּיךָ

בָּרוּךְ
FINAL CHAF

Be Alert!

There are five letters in the Hebrew alphabet that have a different form when they come at the end of a word. When a כ comes at the end of a word, it is a final ך.

When יךָ comes at the end of a word, the י is silent.

89

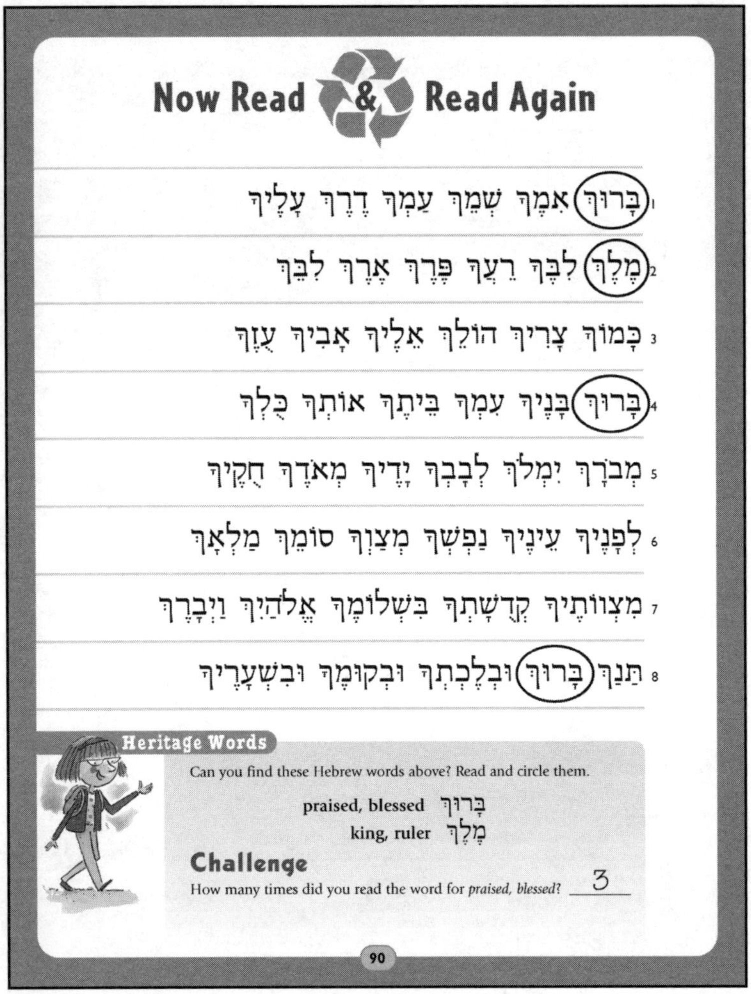

Now Read & Read Again

1 בָּרוּךְ אִמֵּךְ שְׁמֵךְ עַמְךָ דֶּרֶךְ עָלֶיךָ

2 מֶלֶךְ לִבֵּךְ רֵעֵךְ פֶּרֶךְ אֶרֶךְ לִבֵּךְ

3 כָּמוֹךָ צָרִיךְ הוֹלֵךְ אֵלֶיךָ אָבִיךָ עֻזֵּךְ

4 בָּרוּךְ בָּנֶיךָ עִמְּךָ בֵּיתֶךָ אוֹתְךָ כֻּלְּךָ

5 מְבֹרָךְ יִמְלֹךְ לְבָבְךָ יָדֶיךָ מְאֹדֶךָ חֻקֶּיךָ

6 לְפָנֶיךָ עֵינֶיךָ נַפְשְׁךָ מְצַוְּךָ סוֹמֵךְ מַלְאָךְ

7 מִצְווֹתֶיךָ קָדְשָׁתְךָ בִּשְׁלוֹמֶךָ אֱלֹהַיִךְ וַיְבָרֶךְ

8 תַּנֵּךְ בָּרוּךְ וּבְלֶכְתְּךָ וּבְקוּמֶךָ וּבִשְׁעָרֶיךָ

Heritage Words

Can you find these Hebrew words above? Read and circle them.

praised, blessed בָּרוּךְ

king, ruler מֶלֶךְ

Challenge

How many times did you read the word for *praised, blessed*? 3

90

NOW READ & READ AGAIN

Draw a tic-tac-toe grid on the chalkboard. Divide the class into two teams. To place an X or an O on the board, the students must correctly read a line from this page.

HERITAGE WORDS

Name one of the kings of Israel. **[e.g., Saul, David, Solomon]**

Sing the song *David Melech Yisrael.*

PICTURE IT IN HEBREW

Read the word דֶּרֶךְ aloud to the class. Ask students to find the two final letters in the phrase דֶּרֶךְ אֶרֶץ and to give their names and sounds. Then call on individual students to read the paragraph.

Just for Fun: Ask students to make up their own riddles using the word דֶּרֶךְ.

ONLINE WORKBOOK

Assign activities from the online workbook and track your students' progress.

Picture It in Hebrew NEW LETTER ךְ

דֶּרֶךְ

Road

Looking at this דֶּרֶךְ you can see that there is a choice you can make about which way to go. In Hebrew, דֶּרֶךְ means road, but it also means "way"—the way you choose to live. The words דֶּרֶךְ אֶרֶץ tell us about a way to live. Following דֶּרֶךְ אֶרֶץ, literally, "the way of the land," means having good manners and showing respect for others—and for nature.

Q: Why did the rooster cross the דֶּרֶךְ?
A: To prove he wasn't chicken!

בָּרוּךְ אַתָּה, יְיָ אֱלֹהֵינוּ, מֶלֶךְ הָעוֹלָם...
Praised are You, Adonai our God, Ruler of the world...

Put a check next to the בְּרָכוֹת that you read correctly.
Which בְּרָכוֹת do you know?

1 __ הַמּוֹצִיא לֶחֶם מִן הָאָרֶץ. — *who brings forth bread from the earth.*

2 __ בּוֹרֵא פְּרִי הַגָּפֶן. — *who creates the fruit of the vine.*

3 __ בּוֹרֵא פְּרִי הָאֲדָמָה. — *who creates the fruit of the earth.*

4 __ בּוֹרֵא פְּרִי הָעֵץ. — *who creates the fruit of the tree.*

5 __ בּוֹרֵא מִינֵי מְזוֹנוֹת. — *who creates many kinds of food.*

6 __ שֶׁהַכֹּל נִהְיָה בִּדְבָרוֹ. — *by whose word all things come into being.*

7 __ שֶׁהֶחֱיָנוּ וְקִיְּמָנוּ וְהִגִּיעָנוּ לַזְּמַן הַזֶּה. — *for keeping us in life, for sustaining us, and for helping us to reach this day.*

91

LESSON 25

Pages: 92–95
Key Word: אָלֶף
New Letter: ף
Alef-Bet Flashcard: 46
Word Cards: 78, 79

REVIEW EXERCISE

Play the "Grandmother's Suitcase" game as described in #6 on page vii. Use flashcards #1–45. If you are not teaching the names of the vowels, have the students say the vowel sounds.

KEY WORD (אָלֶף)

Point to the *alef* on the *alef-bet* chart and have the students identify it.

Explain that *alef* is the first letter of the Hebrew alphabet. Teach the *Alef-Bet* song to the students and begin to teach the correct order of the letters.

INTRODUCING THE NEW LETTER – ף

At the conclusion of the grandmother's suitcase game you should announce, "I packed my grandmother's suitcase and in it I put a *final fay*." Point out the final *fay* on the *alef-bet* chart and show its location on word card #78. Make sure the students can differentiate between it and the *final chaf*. Ask a volunteer to read the key word from the word card or in the textbook.

READING PRACTICE

Have students work in pairs reading each of the lines to each other. Listen as they practice, and correct any errors that you hear.

NOW READ & READ AGAIN

Have one student read aloud all the Hebrew words on a line, omitting one. Another student reads the Hebrew word that was skipped. This method encourages all the students to pay attention to their classmates reading.

Now Read & Read Again

1 נוֹף הַדַף חַף עָיֵף סַף חוֹף

2 חֹרֶף תֵּיכֶף עֹרֶף עָנָף כֶּסֶף שָׂרַף

3 שֶׁטֶף יוֹסֵף אָלֶף חָלַף כָּתֵף כָּפַף

4 מוּסָף צָפוּף קְלַף זוֹקֵף קוֹטֵף לָעוּף

5 אָסַף נִשְׂרַף שִׁטּוּף רָצוּף כָּנָף יָחֵף

6 עַפְעַף מְרַחֵף רוֹדֵף שָׁלוֹם זוֹקֵף כְּפוּפִים

7 מְצַפְצֵף לְהִתְאַסֵּף לֶאֱסֹף הֶחֱלִיף לְשַׁפְשֵׁף

8 אָלֶף בֵּית וְצִוָּנוּ לְהִתְעַטֵּף בַּצִּיצִית

Heritage Words

Can you find these Hebrew words above? Read and circle them.

alef bet אָלֶף בֵּית *alef* אָלֶף

Challenge

Can you find the Hebrew name for *Joseph* in the lines above?

Write the line number. 3

Do you know the story of Joseph, the son of יַעֲקֹב and רָחֵל?

Can you find the Hebrew word for *peace*? Underline the word.

93

Plant Your Roots

Hebrew words are built on roots.

The word בָּרוּךְ is built on the root ברכ, which means "bless" or "praise."

1. Write one letter—כ, ר, ב—on each of the three roots of the tree, from right to left.
2. Circle the three root letters in each Hebrew word growing on the tree.

Remember!

- The letters ב and בּ are members of the same letter family.
- The letters ך, כ, כּ are members of the same letter family.

Think About It!

What does the root ברכ mean? bless, praise

What would you praise God for in *your* life? ______________________

Challenge

Can you find the Hebrew word for *blessing* in the tree?
Underline the word.

94

PLANT YOUR ROOTS

Make a tree trunk from brown craft paper and post it on your bulletin board. Cut leaf shapes from green construction paper and give one to each student. Tell students to think about something in their lives that they would praise God for and to write it on the leaf. Have students attach their leaves to the bulletin board display.

PICTURE IT IN HEBREW

Have students point to their noses and say the word אַף. Then complete the activity together.

Just for Fun: Ask students to make up short tongue twisters to practice while holding their אַף.

Review: Now that students have learned all the letters in the *alef-bet*, and all the vowels too, review the "Picture It in Hebrew" words on the last page of every chapter in the book. Your students will feel a sense of accomplishment when they discover they can now read all of the words.

RACE CARS

Play "*Alef-Bet* Reading Race." On the board, make a racetrack by writing the *alef-bet* in random order. Call on students to name the letters on the track as quickly as they can, starting on the right. Switch letters around if it becomes too easy.

Option: Use a stopwatch and have students try to beat their own best time.

ONLINE WORKBOOK

Assign activities from the online workbook and track your students' progress.

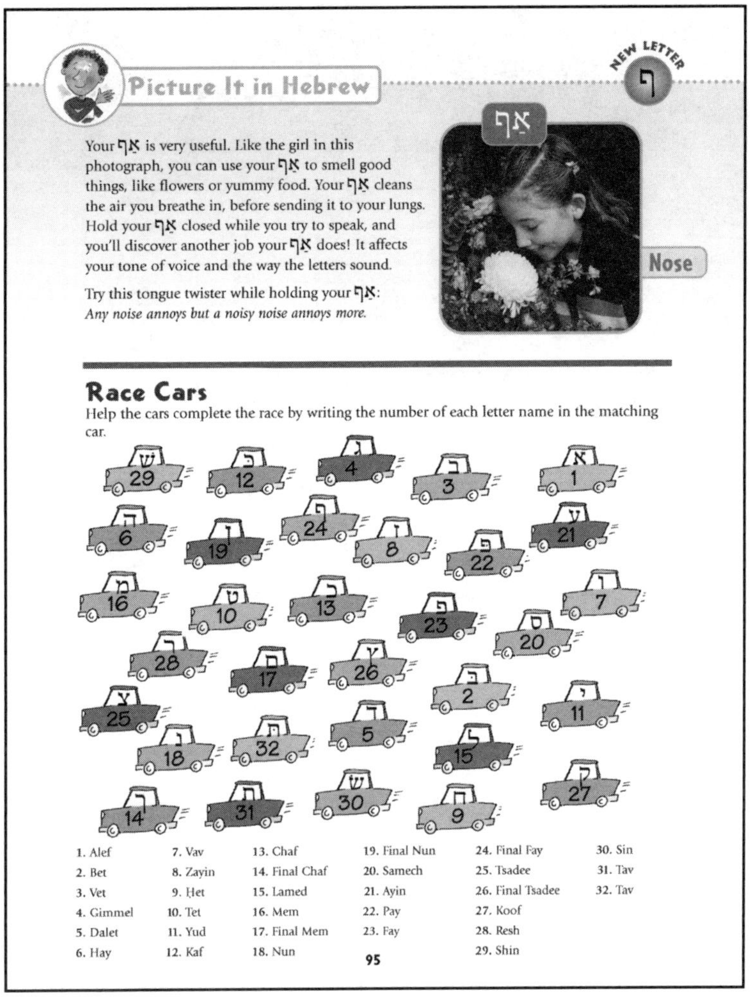

New Letter ף

Picture It in Hebrew

Your אַף is very useful. Like the girl in this photograph, you can use your אַף to smell good things, like flowers or yummy food. Your אַף cleans the air you breathe in, before sending it to your lungs. Hold your אַף closed while you try to speak, and you'll discover another job your אַף does! It affects your tone of voice and the way the letters sound.

Try this tongue twister while holding your אַף:
Any noise annoys but a noisy noise annoys more.

אַף — Nose

Race Cars

Help the cars complete the race by writing the number of each letter name in the matching car.

1. Alef
2. Bet
3. Vet
4. Gimmel
5. Dalet
6. Hay
7. Vav
8. Zayin
9. Het
10. Tet
11. Yud
12. Kaf
13. Chaf
14. Final Chaf
15. Lamed
16. Mem
17. Final Mem
18. Nun
19. Final Nun
20. Samech
21. Ayin
22. Pay
23. Fay
24. Final Fay
25. Tsadee
26. Final Tsadee
27. Koof
28. Resh
29. Shin
30. Sin
31. Tav
32. Tav

95

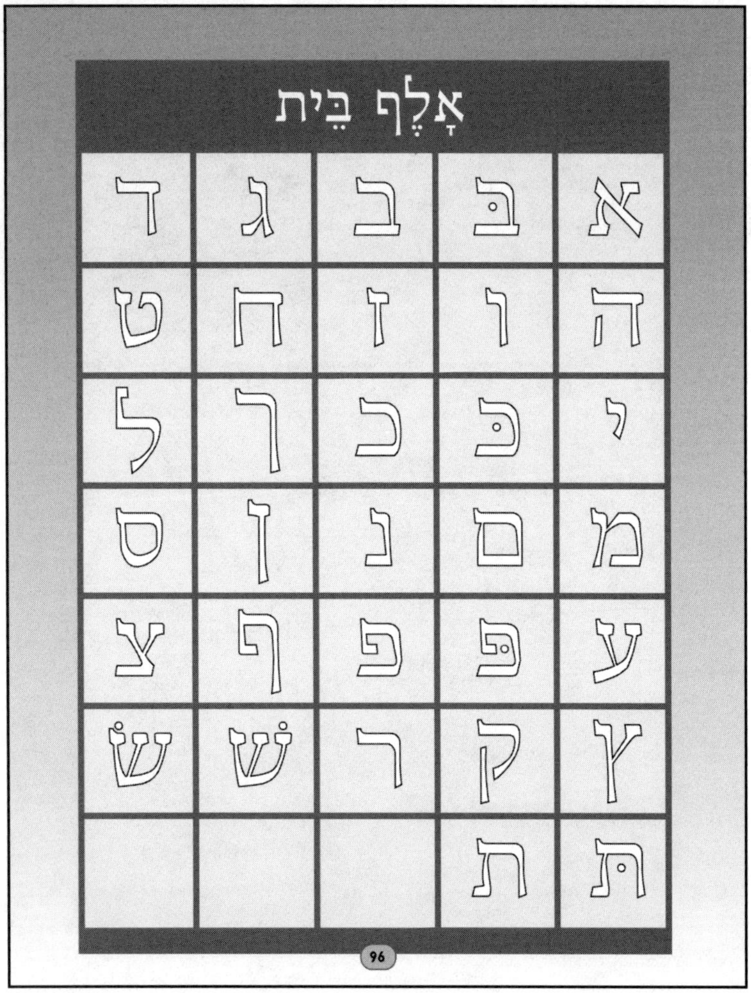

אָלֶף בֵּית

ד	ג	ב	בּ	א
ט	ח	ז	ו	ה
ל	ך	כ	כּ	י
ס	ן	נ	ם	מ
צ	ף	פ	פּ	ע
שׂ	שׁ	ר	ק	ץ
			ת	תּ

96